World Geography Terms
Human Geography and Physical Geography

Kenneth Ma & Jennifer Fu

Geography Collections

All rights reserved. No part of this publication may be reproduced, distributed, or transmitted in any form or by any means, or stored in a database or retrieval system, without written permission.

Write to geopublish@gmail.com for more information about this book.

Book Title:	World Geography Terms
	Human Geography and Physical Geography
Author:	Kenneth Ma & Jennifer Fu
ISBN-10:	1466329068
ISBN-13:	978-1466329065

Table of Contents

Introduction 1

Human Geography Terms 2

    Administrative Division 2

    Canal 2

    Capital 2

    City 3

    Country 4

    Culture 4

    Currency 5

    Dam 5

    Ethnic Group 6

    Exclusive Economic Zone 6

    Government 6

    National Anthem 7

    National Park 7

    Religion 8

    Reservoir 8

Physical Geography Terms 10

    Ablation 10

    Ablation Zone 10

    Abrasion 10

    Abyssal Fan 10

    Abyssal Plain 10

    Accumulation 11

    Accumulation Zone 11

    Air Current 11

    Alluvial Fan 12

    Anabranch 12

    Antipode 12

    Arch 12

    Archipelago 12

    Arête 13

    Arroyo 14

    Atoll 14

Ayre	14
Badland	14
Backwash	14
Barchan Dune	15
Barrier Island	15
Bay	15
Bayou	15
Beach	16
Beach Cusp	16
Beach Ridge	16
Bedrock	17
Bench	17
Bight	17
Bill	17
Biome	17
Biosphere	18
Blowout Depression	18
Blowhole	19
Braided Stream	19
Butte	19
Caldera	19
Calving	20
Canyon	20
Cape	21
Cave	22
Channel	23
Cirque	24
Cliff	24
Climate	27
Cloud	27
Coastal Plain	28
Cold Seep	28
Continental Crust	28
Continental Divide	28
Continental Drift	29
Continental Margin	29
Continental Rise	30

Continental Shelf	30
Continental Slope	30
Coral Reef	30
Cove	31
Crater Lake	31
Crevasse	33
Crevice	33
Cuesta	33
Cuspate Foreland	33
Delta	33
Desert	35
Desert Pavement	35
Desert Varnish	36
Dissected Plateau	36
Drainage Divide	36
Dreikanter	36
Drumlin	36
Dry Lake	36
Dune	37
Earthquake	37
El Niño	37
Endorheic Basin	38
Eolianite	38
Erosion	38
Erg	38
Escarpment	38
Esker	39
Estuary	39
Exhumed River Channel	40
Fault	40
Firn	40
Firth	40
Fjord	41
Flood Basalt	41
Floodplain	42
Fluvial terrace	42
Forest	42

Geyser	43
Glacier	44
Glacier Cave	44
Gulch	45
Gulf	45
Gully	45
Headland	46
Hill	46
Hogback	46
Hoodoo	46
Hydrosphere	46
Iceberg	46
Inlet	46
Island	47
Island Arc	47
Isthmus	47
Kame	49
Karst	49
Kettle	49
Lacustrine Plain	50
Lagoon	50
Lake	50
Landform	52
Landslide	53
La Niña	54
Latitude	54
Lava	54
Lava Channel	54
Lava Dome	54
Lava Flow	55
Lavaka	55
Lava Lake	55
Lava Plain	55
Lava Spine	55
Lava Tube	55
Limestone Pavement	56
Loess	56

Longitude	56
Longshore Current	56
Longshore Drift	57
Longshore Transport	57
Maar	57
Machair	57
Malpais	57
Mamelon	57
Marsh	58
Mass Wasting	58
Meander	58
Mesa	58
Mid-Ocean Ridge	58
Mineral	59
Mineraloid	60
Monadnock	60
Moraine	61
Moulin	61
Mountain	61
Névé	63
Nivation	63
Oasis	63
Ocean	64
Ocean Basin	64
Oceanic crust	65
Oceanic Plateau	65
Oceanic Trench	65
Oxbow Lake	66
Pediment	66
Peneplain	66
Peninsula	66
Pingo	66
Pit Crater	67
Plain	67
Playa	67
Plateau	67
Point	68

Pond 68

Potrero 68

Proglacial Lake 68

Promontory 69

Pseudocrater 69

Pyramidal Peak 69

Rainforest 69

Rapid 69

Ravine 69

Reef 69

Ria 70

Ridge 70

Rift Valley 70

River 70

Roche Moutonnée 72

Rock 72

Sandhill 73

Salt Marsh 73

Scree 73

Sea 73

Sea Cave 75

Sediment 75

Serac 75

Shoal 75

Sinkhole 75

Snowfield 76

Snow Line 76

Sound 76

Spit 76

Spring 76

Stack 78

Strait 78

Stratum 79

Stump 79

Subglacial Mound 79

Submarine Canyon 79

Surge Channel 79

Swamp 80

Swash 81

Table 81

Tea Table 81

Tepui 81

Terrace 82

Topography 82

Tornado 82

Tombolo 82

Tropical Cyclone 83

Tuya 83

Vale 83

Valley 83

Ventifact 85

Volcanic Arc 85

Volcanic Complex 85

Volcanic Cone 87

Volcanic Crater 87

Volcanic Dam 88

Volcanic Field 88

Volcano 89

Waterfall 90

Water Salinity 92

Watershed 92

Wave-Cut Platform 92

Wetland 92

Wind 92

Yardang 93

Bibliography 94

Other Books 95

About the Authors 96

Introduction

As a young child, I always enjoyed looking at maps to better understand the world around me. When I heard of the National Geography Bee, I finally got a chance to put it into use. During the contest, I realized how there wasn't just one study guide that covered the entire world effectively. After the contest was over, I thought that the people who had to compete after me shouldn't have to go through the same pain studying from tons of different study guides as well as helping those who simply want to learn more about the world. This got me started on this series of books.

This book is the sixth one of the World Geography Series. This book is slightly different from the previous books, as it covers general geographical terms. This book is not written in a questionnaire format, but rather as a type of glossary so that it is easier to learn what the terms mean.

If you have any questions or comments, please send email to geopublish@gmail.com.

This book would have never been possible without the help of my parents, especially my mom, who is also my co-author, my teachers, and my sister. Many thanks to my parents for encouraging me and pushing me to go on, my teacher, Mr. Blair, for starting and widening my interest for geography, and my sister, Hermione, who helped me find the information and get to know it better.

Kenneth Ma

Human Geography Terms

Human geography is the branch of geography that studies the human use and interaction of the world. This includes things such as culture, development, historic, and other human issues.

Administrative Division

An administrative division is a portion of the country that has its own local government. The administrative divisions of a country can be called by different names depending on the country. There can be smaller administrative divisions within an administrative division.

Common names for administrative divisions are:

- Department – used by some countries including Argentina, France, Niger, Peru, and Senegal. Can be used as a smaller administrative division.
- District – used by some countries including Austria, Canada, Germany, and Japan. Districts are usually the names for smaller administrative districts.
- Division – used by some countries including Bangladesh, India, Malaysia, and Pakistan.
- State – used by some countries including Myanmar, Palau, and the United States.
- Province – used by most countries including Afghanistan, Canada, Italy, Spain, Turkey, and Vietnam.

Canal

A canal is a man-made channel for water.

Types of canals:

- Transport – built to allow ships a shorter travel. Some examples are the Panama Canal in Panama and the Suez Canal in Egypt.
- Water supply – built to transport water to a country's populations.

Capital

A capital is the city that houses the government of the region. Because of its importance, it is often the most famous city of the country. There are usually capital cities in all administrative divisions. In some cases, there is more than one capital city as the branches of government are housed in different locations.

Some capital cities do not house the government:

- Porto Novo – capital of Benin, but government buildings are located in Cotonou.
- Sucre – one of the capitals of Bolivia, but the government has moved to the other

capital La Paz.
- Yamoussoukro – one of the capitals of Côte d'Ivoire, but most government buildings are in Abidjan.
- Amsterdam – capital of the Netherlands, but government buildings are located in The Hague.

Cities that house parts of the government but are not designated as a capital:

- Valparaíso – houses Chile's Congress. Chile's capital is Santiago.
- Brno – houses Czech Republic's high court. Czech Republic's capital is Prague.
- Versailles – joint meetings of the Parliament take place in Versailles instead of France's capital Paris.
- Bonn/Karlsruhe/Kassel/Leipzig – houses several ministries and the judicial branch of Germany. The capital of Germany is Berlin.
- Lausanne – houses the Supreme Court of Switzerland. The capital of Switzerland is Bern.
- Putrajaya – houses the federal administration of Malaysia. The capital of Malaysia is Kuala Lumpur.
- Yangoon – houses most government buildings of Myanmar. The capital of Myanmar was moved to Naypyidaw in 2005.
- Dar es Salaam – houses most government buildings of Tanzania. The capital of Tanzania is Dodoma.
- Colombo – houses most government buildings of Sri Lanka. The capital of Sri Lanka is Sri Jayewardenepura Kotte.

City

A city is a large permanent settlement. Settlements usually are classified as a city if they have a fairly large population or have some government functions for the surrounding regions.

A city typically includes the surrounding suburbs in addition to the central city. With all the areas combined, it is known as the metropolitan area.

Largest cities by population (metro area) in the world:

- Tokyo – the most populous city in the world and is the capital and a prefecture of Japan.
- Seoul – the 2nd most populous city in the world and is the capital of South Korea.
- Shanghai – the 3rd most populous city in the world. It is located in China.
- Guangzhou – the 4th most populous city in the world. It is located in China.
- Karachi – the 5th most populous city in the world. It is located in Pakistan.
- Delhi – the 6th most populous city in the world. It contains the capital of India, New Delhi.
- Mexico City – the 7th most populous city in the world and is the capital of Mexico. It

is also the most populous city in the Americas.
- Beijing – the 8th most populous city in the world and is the capital of China.
- Lagos- the 9th most populous city in the world and is the capital of Nigeria.
- São Paulo – the 10th most populous city in the world. It is located in Brazil.

Country

A country is a geographic region and is usually sovereign. There are currently 204 countries in the world, but only 195 of them are officially recognized by the United Nations.

There are several countries that claim to be independent but are not widely recognized as independent:

- Abkhazia – an autonomous region in northwestern Azerbaijan. Recognized only by Russia, Nauru, Nicaragua, Vanuatu, Venezuela, South Ossetia (not recognized as a country), and Transnistria (not recognized as a country).
- Nagorno–Karabakh – a de facto independent republic in southwestern Azerbaijan. It has power over itself but is not officially recognized by anyone but Transnistria (not recognized as a country). Peace talks are currently happening between Armenia and Azerbaijan over the fate of the region.
- Northern Cyprus – a de facto independent state located on the northern half of Cyprus. It is only recognized by Turkey.
- Palestine – comprised of the regions of West Bank and Gaza Strip. Its independence has been in dispute ever since the creation of Israel in 1948 and it declared independence in 1988. It is currently recognized by over 80 countries.
- Sahrawi Arab Democratic Republic – a partially recognized republic which claims Western Sahara, currently run by Morocco. It is recognized by 82 other countries, and some other countries had recognized the republic before revoking it.
- Somaliland – a de facto independent state on the northern half of Somalia. It is not recognized as an independent country.
- South Ossetia – a de facto independent state in northern Georgia. It is recognized by Russia, Nicaragua, Nauru, Venezuela, Abkhazia (not recognized as a country) and Transnistria (not recognized as a country).
- Taiwan – a sovereign state that claims and is claimed by the People's Republic of China. There are 23 countries that recognize the island of Taiwan, and it has been a member of the United Nations in the past.
- Transnistria – a de facto state comprising of a strip of land on the northeastern border of Moldova and Ukraine in Moldova. It is recognized by Abkhazia (not recognized as a country) and South Ossetia (not recognized as a country)

Culture

Culture is a set of shared values and goals by a group of people. Culture is usually separated by place of origin, though other factors such as language and current geography can also create a whole new set of culture.

Currency

Currency is used as by countries as a medium of exchange. Countries typically have different currencies though there are some countries that have the same currency and others with the same name.

Common currency names (countries with the same currency have the currency name in parenthesis):

- Dinar – used by Algeria, Bahrain, Iraq, Jordan, Kuwait, Libya, Serbia, and Tunisia.
- Dollar– used by Antigua Barbuda (East Caribbean Dollar), Australia (Australian Dollar), Belize, Bahamas, Barbados, Belize, Brunei, Canada, Dominica (East Caribbean Dollar), East Timor (US Dollar), Ecuador (US Dollar), El Salvador (US Dollar), Fiji, Grenada (East Caribbean Dollar), Guyana, Hong Kong, Jamaica, Kiribati, Liberia, Marshall Islands (US Dollar), Federated States of Micronesia (US Dollar), Namibia, Nauru (Australian Dollar), New Zealand, Palau (US Dollar), Saint Kitts and Nevis (East Caribbean Dollar), Saint Lucia (East Caribbean Dollar), Saint Vincent and the Grenadines (East Caribbean Dollar), Singapore, Solomon Islands, Suriname, Taiwan, Trinidad and Tobago, Tuvalu, United States (US Dollar), Zimbabwe (US Dollar).
- Euro – used by Austria, Belgium, Cyprus, Estonia, Finland, France, Germany, Greece, Ireland, Italy, Luxembourg, Malta, Netherlands, Portugal, Slovakia, Slovenia, and Spain.
- Franc – used by Benin (West CFA Franc), Burkina Faso (West CFA Franc), Burundi, Cameroon (CFA Franc) , Central African Republic (CFA Franc), Chad (CFA Franc), Comoros, Republic of the Congo (CFA Franc), Democratic Republic of the Congo, Côte d'Ivoire (West CFA Franc), Djibouti, Equatorial Guinea (CFA Franc), Gabon (CFA Franc), Guinea, Guinea-Bissau (West CFA Franc), Mali (West CFA Franc), Niger (West CFA Franc), Rwanda, Senegal (West CFA Franc), Switzerland, and Togo (West CFA Franc).
- Peso – Argentina, Chile, Colombia, Cuba, Dominican Republic, Mexico, Philippines, and Uruguay.
- Pound – used by Egypt, Lebanon, Sudan, South Sudan, Syria, and the United Kingdom.
- Rupee – used by India, Mauritania, Nepal, Pakistan, Seychelles, and Sri Lanka.

Other major currencies:

- Real – used by Brazil.
- Yen – used by Japan.
- Yuan – used by China.

Dam

A dam is a structure that acts as a barrier for water. Dams are mostly built to protect an area from flooding by blocking the water, although they are also built to generate hydroelectricity. A dam usually causes a reservoir before the area as it is blocked, which can cause human population displacement. The Three Gorges Dam in China is the largest dam in the world.

Ethnic Group
An ethnic group is a group of people with similar culture. There are several general major ethnic groups that now exist worldwide: Caucasian, Latino, Asian, Black, and Mixed. Ethnic groups also exist in more specific terms, but those vary greatly by country.

Exclusive Economic Zone
An Exclusive Economic Zone is a sea zone where a particular country has special rights. These rights include scientific purposes such as exploration as well as economic purposes such as fishing and drilling for oil. An Exclusive Economic Zone usually stretches out 200 mi (322 km) from its sea border, though it will be less if different Exclusive Economic Zones would overlap.

Areas of dispute:

- Rockall – island in the North Atlantic Ocean claimed by Iceland, Denmark, Ireland and the United Kingdom. Whoever Rockall belongs to also would have the rights to the ocean around it.
- Spratly Islands – island in the South China Sea claimed by Brunei, Malaysia, Philippines, China, Taiwan, and Vietnam.
- Beaufort Sea – part of the sea is claimed by both Canada and US because of possible oil reserves in that region.
- Saint Pierre and Miquelon – belongs to France, the region around the island is claimed by Canada.

Countries with the largest Exclusive Economic Zones:

- United States (4,382,645 sq mi / 11,351,000 km²)
- France (4,260,000 sq mi / 11,035,000 km²)
- Australia (3,146,056 sq mi / 8,148,250 km²)
- Russia (2,921,508 sq mi / 7,566,673 km²)
- the United Kingdom (2,627,651 sq mi / 6,805,586 km²)
- New Zealand (2,580,128 sq mi/6,682,503 km²)
- Indonesia (2,378,015 sq mi / 6,159,032 km²)
- Canada (2,161,815 sq mi /5,599,077 km²)
- Japan (1,729,501 sq mi / 4,479,388 km²)
- Chile (1,421,623 sq mi / 3,681,989 km²)

Government
A government is a group of legislators, administrators, and other officials who control a

state. They determine policies in the state and how to enforce them.

Types of government:

- Anarchism – believes in almost no government. Currently there is no state run by anarchy, though anarchists start many riots worldwide.
- Authoritarian – believes in power to the government. Usually the leaders of an authoritarian state will be appointed rather than elected, but they still grant limited personal freedom. There is currently no state that is under authoritarian rule.
- Constitutional Monarchy – has a government ruled by a king by its constitution, but with many restrictions. The United Kingdom has a Constitutional Monarchy, and has a queen yet is mostly ruled by the prime minister and the Parliament.
- Constitutional Republic – has a government where all laws and matters are made by a vote. Ancient Greece had this type of government, but at this moment there is no true republic.
- Democracy – a type of republic where the population votes for a representative in which to make laws and policy. Democracy is ruled by a majority. Currently, many countries in the world use this system of government. Notable examples include France and the United States.
- Dictatorship – rule by one person. Currently the most common dictatorship is a military dictatorship, where the general of the nation's army seized power and is the sole person in power. Libya is an example of a military dictatorship.
- Monarchy – a government that is ruled by the king. Most monarchies have been overthrown, but some still exist, such as Bahrain, Brunei, Oman, Qatar, Saudi Arabia and Swaziland.
- Oligarchy – a government that is ruled by a few individuals. Oligarchy now most often occurs in the corporate world rather than the government.
- Plutocracy – a government where the rich rule. All democracies are a plutocracy to an extent because the rich have influence over many politicians' votes.
- Theocracy – a government is ruled by the religious elite. There are some theocracies in the world, such as Vatican City and many Muslim countries in Africa and the Middle East.
- Totalitarian – a government that controls every aspect of its citizens' life. There is no complete totalitarian government at the present. Nazi Germany and Stalin Soviet Union are examples of totalitarian government in the past.

National Anthem
A national anthem is a patriotic song that glorifies the country's history and/or traditions. It is recognized by the country's government as the official national song of that country.

National Park
A national park is a region that is protected by the government from most development. The point of a national park is to protect the unique environment that the region houses. Yellowstone National Park in the United States was the first national park in the world,

gaining the status on March 1st, 1872.

Religion

Religion is a system of cultural beliefs that usually have to do with spirituality. Most countries in the world do not have an official religion, except for some Islamic countries in the Middle East.

Major religions of the world:

- Christianity – predominant in most regions of the world (except for the regions where another religion is predominant).
- Islam – predominant in the Middle East and northern Africa.
- Buddhism – predominant in eastern Asia.
- Hinduism – predominant in India.

Reservoir

A reservoir is an artificial lake that stores water. Reservoirs are created by dams or by excavation.

Types of reservoirs:

- Valley dammed reservoir – a reservoir created by a dam. The dam is usually put at the narrowest point of the river valley, so the water will fan out into a reservoir. Its size depends largely on the size of the valley.
- Bank side reservoir – a reservoir created by siphoning or pumping water from a river.

Largest reservoirs in the world:

- Lake Volta – a large reservoir in Ghana created by the Akosombo Dam. It is the largest reservoir in the world by surface area (3,283 sq mi / 8,502 km^2), and the 4th largest reservoir by volume (36 cu mi / 148 km^3).
- Smallwood Reservoir – a large reservoir in eastern Canada created by numerous dikes. It is the 2nd largest reservoir in the world by surface area (2,520 sq mi / 6,527 km²).
- Kuybyshev Reservoir – a large reservoir in western Russia created by the Zhiguli Hydroelectric Station Dam. It is the 3rd largest reservoir in the world by surface area (2,490 sq mi / 6,450 km²).
- Lake Kariba – a large reservoir in Zimbabwe and Zambia created by the Kariba Dam. It is the 4th largest reservoir in the world by surface area (2,150 sq mi / 5,580 km²), and the largest reservoir by volume (43 cu mi / 180 km^3).
- Buhktarma Reservoir – a large reservoir in Kazakhstan created by the Bukhtarma Hydroelectric Dam. It is the 5th largest reservoir in the world by surface area (2,120 sq mi / 5,490 km²).

- Bratsk Reservoir – a large reservoir in southern Russia created by the Bratsk hydroelectric dam. It is the 6th largest reservoir in the world by surface area (2,095 sq mi / 5,426 km²), and the 2nd largest reservoir by volume (41 cu mi / 169 km³).
- Lake Nasser – a large reservoir in Egypt and Sudan created by the Aswan Dam. It is the 7th largest reservoir in the world by surface area (2,026 sq mi / 5,248 km²), and the 3rd largest reservoir by volume (38 cu mi / 157 km³).
- Rybinsk Reservoir – a large reservoir in western Russia created by the Rybinsk Hydroelectric Dam. It is the 8th largest reservoir in the world by surface area (1,770 sq mi / 4,580 km²).

Physical Geography Terms

Physical geography is the branch of geography that has to deal with the natural environment, such as atmosphere and landscape. It does not deal with things that have been modified by humans in any way.

Ablation
Ablation refers to all processes that remove snow, ice, or water from a glacier or snowfield. It is the opposite of accumulation. It can refer either to the processes removing ice and snow or to the quantity of ice and snow removed. Ablation is also sometimes used to describe general erosion.

Ablation Zone
An ablation zone is a region of the glacier where it loses part of its ice and snow by melting, sublimation or calving. An ablation zone is the opposite of an accumulation zone. The ablation zones are located in almost all glaciers.

Abrasion
Abrasion is the physical scraping of a rock surface by friction between rocks and other moving particles caused by wind, glacier, waves, gravity, running water or other forms of erosion.

Abyssal Fan
An abyssal fan is a fan shaped deposit created at the end of rivers. Abyssal fans are always underwater, which are also thought of as an underwater version of alluvial fans. There are Abyssal fans formed at the ends of many large rivers, such as the Mississippi River and the Nile River.

Abyssal Plain
An abyssal plain is an underwater plain on the deep ocean floor. Abyssal plains cover more than 50% of the Earth's surface.

Major abyssal plains in the world:

- South Atlantic Ocean – Angola Abyssal Plain, Argentine Abyssal Plain, Burdwood Abyssal Plain, Cape Abyssal Plain, Fernando de Noronha Abyssal Plain, Namibia Abyssal Plain, Pernambuco Abyssal Plain, and Town Abyssal Plain
- North Atlantic Ocean – Adriatic Abyssal Plain, Alaskan Abyssal Plain, Alboran Abyssal Plain, Balearic Abyssal Plain, Bering Abyssal Plain, Cascadia Abyssal Plain, Ceara Abyssal Plain, Clark Abyssal Plain, Colombian Abyssal Plain, Eratosthenes Abyssal Plain, Euxine Abyssal Plain, Florida Abyssal Plain, Grenada Abyssal Plain, Herodotus Abyssal Plain, Jamaican Abyssal Plain, Messina Abyssal Plain, Norway

Abyssal Plain, Rhodes Abyssal Plain, Sardino-Balearic Abyssal Plain, Sierra Leone Abyssal Plain, Sigsbee Abyssal Plain, Sirte Abyssal Plain, Tyrrhenian Abyssal Plain, Venezuela Abyssal Plain, and Yucatan Abyssal Plain
- Southern Ocean – Amundsen Abyssal Plain, Bellingshausen Abyssal Plain, Enderby Abyssal Plain, South Indian Abyssal Plain, Valdivia Abyssal Plain, and Wendell Abyssal Plain
- Arctic Ocean – Boreas Abyssal Plain, Canada Abyssal Plain, Chukchi Abyssal Plain, Dumshaf Abyssal Plain, Fletcher Abyssal Plain, Barents Abyssal Plain, Greenland Abyssal Plain, Mendeleyev Abyssal Plain, Northwind Abyssal Plain, Pole Abyssal Plain, Siberian Abyssal Plain, and Wrangel Abyssal Plain
- Indian Ocean – Ceylon Abyssal Plain, Cocos Abyssal Plain, Comores Abyssal Plain, Cuvier Abyssal Plain, Gascoyne Abyssal Plain, Malagasy Abyssal Plain, Mid Indian Abyssal Plain, Argo Abyssal Plain, Oman Abyssal Plain, Perth Abyssal Plain, Somali Abyssal Plain, and South Australian Abyssal Plain
- Southern Ocean – Enderby Abyssal Plain, South Indian Abyssal Plain, Valdivia Abyssal Plain, and Weddell Abyssal Plain
- Pacific Ocean – Bering Abyssal Plain, Cascadia Abyssal Plain, Japan Abyssal Plain, Mornington Abyssal Plain, Okhotsk Abyssal Plain, Papua Abyssal Plain, Raukumara Abyssal Plain, South China Sea Abyssal Plain, South West Pacific Abyssal Plain, and Tasman Abyssal Plain

Accumulation
Accumulation refers to all processes that add snow to a glacier or snowfield.

Accumulation Zone
An accumulation zone is a region of the glacier where it gains snow. The accumulation zone is the opposite of the ablation zone. The accumulation zones are located in almost all glaciers, which are most commonly found towards the northern part of Earth.

Air Current
Air currents are currents of moving air caused by differences in atmosphere, temperature, or pressure.

There are three major types of air currents:

- Advection turning – an air current caused by the difference of temperature. The current will turn clockwise if the current goes from warm to cold air and vice versa.
- Frontogenesis – caused by a difference in temperature which will strengthen air currents.
- Jet stream – a fast thin air current in the troposphere. Most jet streams tend to go from west to east. They are caused by the rotation of Earth as well as the temperature differences on the Earth's surface due to the way that solar heat reaches different points on Earth.

Alluvial Fan

An alluvial fan is a fan shaped deposit created when a fast flowing stream slows and spreads out. Alluvial fans are created mainly due to an increase of space provided for the water to flow through.

Anabranch

An anabranch is a section of a river or stream that diverts from the main channel or stem of the watercourse and rejoins the main stem downstream. There are anabranches at the junction of the Yukon River and the Koyukuk River in Alaska, the United States.

Antipode

Antipode is the point on the opposite side of Earth of the selected point. Usually, the antipode of land will be a point on water.

Biggest antipodal land overlaps:

- Malay Peninsula – Amazon Basin
- Mongolia and East China – Argentina and Chile

Arch

An arch is a natural geological formation where a rock arch forms, with an opening underneath. An arch is also called a natural arch, a bridge, or a natural bridge. Many arches in Arches National Park and Rainbow Bridge National Monument of Utah, the United States, are weather-eroded arches. The arches in Natural Bridges National Monument of Utah, the United States, are water-eroded arches. The London Arch in Port Campbell National Park, Australia, was formed from the cave erosion. Due to the continuing erosion, it collapsed unexpectedly on January 15th, 1990.

Archipelago

An archipelago is a group of islands that are usually of volcanic origin.

Largest archipelagos by area in the world:

- Malay Archipelago – an archipelago in the Indian and Pacific Ocean that includes the countries of Brunei, East Timor, Indonesia, Malaysia, Papua New Guinea, Philippines, and Singapore. The area of the islands totals around 800,000 sq mi / 2,000,000 km^2.
- Canadian Arctic Archipelago – an archipelago in the Arctic Ocean that makes up the territory of Nunavut in Canada. The area of the islands totals around 303,396 sq mi / 1,424,500 km^2.
- Japanese archipelago – an archipelago in the Pacific Ocean that contains all of the islands of Japan. The area of the islands totals around 145,886 sq mi / 377,944 km^2.
- British Isles – an archipelago in the Atlantic Ocean that makes up all of the United

- Kingdom as well as Ireland. The area of the islands totals around 121,674 sq mi / 315,134 km^2.
- New Zealand – an archipelago in the Pacific Ocean that contains the country of New Zealand. The area of the islands totals around 103,483 sq mi / 268,021 km^2.
- Antilles – an archipelago in the Caribbean Sea. The Antilles contain two sub archipelagos, the Greater Antilles and the Lesser Antilles. The Great Antilles includes the countries of Bahamas, Cuba, Dominican Republic, Haiti, and Jamaica. The Lesser Antilles makes up the countries of Antigua and Barbuda, Barbados, Dominica, Grenada, Saint Kitts and Nevis, Saint Lucia, Saint Vincent and the Grenadines, and Trinidad and Tobago. The area of the islands totals around 81,060 sq mi / 210,000 km^2.

Largest archipelagos by number of islands in the world:

- Archipelago Sea – a sea between Finland and Sweden that contain a total of about 50,000 islands.
- Canadian Arctic Archipelago in the Arctic Ocean – contains 36,563 islands.
- Malay Archipelago in the Indian and Pacific Ocean – contains between 25,000 and 30,000 (includes Indonesia and Philippines) islands.
- Stockholm Archipelago in the Baltic Sea – contains about 24,000 islands.
- Japanese archipelago in the Pacific Ocean – contains 6,852 islands.
- Antilles in the Caribbean Sea – contains 3,515 islands.

Largest island countries by area in the world:

- Indonesia – the largest island country in the world and comprises of 13,466 islands.
- Japan – the 2nd largest island country in the world and comprises of 6,852 islands.
- Philippines – the 3rd largest island country in the world and comprises of 7,107 islands.
- New Zealand – the 4th largest island country in the world and comprises of 33 islands.
- United Kingdom – the 5th largest island country in the world and comprises of 2 main islands and many smaller isles.

Arête

An arête is a thin ridge of rock formed when glaciers carve valleys on both sides of the rock. An arête consists of only two glaciers carving parallel.

Arêtes examples:

- Knife Edge in Maine, the United States
- Clouds Rest in California, the United States
- The Minarets in California, the United States
- The Garden Wall in Montana, the United States

- The Sawtooth in the Colorado Rockies, the United States
- La Peineta, Chile
- Crib Goch, the United Kingdom
- Striding Edge, the United Kingdom
- The Catwalk in Washington, the United States
- The Carn Mor Dearg Arête, the United Kingdom

Arroyo

An arroyo is a dry river, creek, or stream bed which is usually dry except after heavy rain. An arroyo is a dry gulch. An arroyo is a rambla, or a wadi. Arroyos can be natural fluvial landforms or constructed flood control channels. The Arroyo Seco and the Los Angeles River of California are examples of former natural arroyo seasonal watercourses that became constructed open drainage system arroyos.

Atoll

An atoll is an island (or islands) of coral that partially or completely encircles a lagoon. Most of atolls are in the Pacific Ocean and the Indian Ocean. The largest atoll by total area is the Saya de Malha Bank in the Indian Ocean (13,513 sq mi / 35,000 km²).

Ayre

An ayre is a body of water divided from the sea by a narrow bar of land. Sometimes, ayre is used interchangeable with tombolo. The Vasa Loch and the Lairo Water in the Orkney Islands of Scotland are ayres.

Badland

A badland is a type of dry terrain where softer sedimentary rocks and clay-rich soils have been extensively eroded by wind and water. Canyons, ravines, gullies, hoodoos are common in badlands.

Badland examples:

- Makoshika State Park in Montana, the United States
- Theodore Roosevelt National Park in North Dakota, the United States
- Badlands National Park in South Dakota, the United States
- Toadstool Geologic Park in Nebraska, the United States
- Dinosaur National Monument in Colorado and Utah, the United States
- Big Muddy Badlands in Canada
- Dinosaur Provincial Park in Canada
- Royal Tyrrell Museum of Paleontology in Canada
- Putangirua Pinnacles in New Zealand
- Bardenas Reales in Spain

Backwash

Backwash is a seaward current that results from the receding swash on the beach face, after a wave breaks.

Barchan Dune
A barchan dune is an arc-shaped sand ridge, comprised of well-sorted sand. Great Sand Dunes National Park in Colorado, the United States, has spectacular examples of barchan dunes.

Barrier Island
Barrier Island is a type of barrier system, which usually occurs in chains, consisting of anything from a few islands to more than a dozen. Barrier Islands are relatively narrow strips of sand that parallel the mainland coast. The Mississippi-Alabama barrier islands lie outside Mobile Bay in Alabama and Mississippi Sound in Mississippi, the United States.

Bay
Bay is an area of water mostly surrounded by land. A small bay is called a cove, and a large bay is called a gulf, a sea, a sound, or a bight.

Largest bays by area in the world:

- Bay of Bengal – the largest bay in the world (838,613 sq mi / 2,172,000 km²). It is located in the Indian Ocean.
- Hudson's Bay – the 2nd largest bay in the world (470,000 sq mi / 1,230,000 sq km²). It is located in Canada.
- Baffin Bay – the 3rd largest bay in the world (266,000 sq mi / 689,000 km²). It is located between Canada and Greenland.
- Chesapeake Bay – the 4th largest bay in the world (64,299 sq mi / 166,534 km²). It is located in the United States.
- James Bay – the 5th largest bay in the world (42,460 sq mi / 110,000 km²). It is located in Canada.
- Bay of Fundy – the 6th largest bay in the world (3,590 sq mi / 9,300 km²). It is located in Canada.
- Port Phillip Bay – the 6th largest bay in the world (750 sq mi / 1,930 km²). It is located in Australia.
- San Francisco Bay – the 7th largest bay in the world (from 400 sq mi / 1,040 km² to 1,600 sq mi / 4,160 km², depending whether to include sub-bays, estuaries, and wetlands), It is located in California, the United States.
- Banderas Bay – the 8th largest bay in the world (618 sq mi / 1,600 km²). It is located in Mexico.

Bayou
A bayou is a body of water typically found in flat, low-lying areas, and can refer either to an extremely slow-moving stream or river, or to a marshy lake or wetland. Bayou

Bartholomew, located in Arkansas and Louisiana, the United States, is the longest bayou in the world (375 mi / 604 km). Bayous are commonly found in the Gulf Coast region of the southern United States, such as Bayou Lafourche, Bayou Teche, and Bayou Saint John in Louisiana, Cypress Bayou and Buffalo Bayou in Texas, and Big Bayou Canot and Bayou La Batre in Alabama.

Beach

A beach is the landform along the shoreline of an ocean, sea, or lake. It usually consists of loose particles, such as sand, gravel, shingle, pebbles, or cobblestones by the action of breaking waves.

Longest beaches in the world:

- Praia do Cassino – the longest beach in the world (158 mi / 254 km). It is located in Brazil.
- Cox's Bazar – the 2nd longest beach in the world (150 mi / 241 km). It is located in Bangladesh.
- Padre Island – the 3rd longest beach in the world (130 mi / 209 km). It is located in Texas, the United States.
- Ninety Mile Beach (Australia) – the 4th longest beach in the world (90 mi / 145 km). It is located in Australia.
- Ninety Mile Beach (New Zealand) – the 5th longest beach in the world (88 mi / 142 km). It is located in New Zealand.
- Playa Novillero – the 6th longest beach in the world (51 mi / 82 km). It is located in Mexico.
- Virginia Beach – the 7th longest beach in the world (35 mi / 56 km). It is located in Virginia, the United States.
- Long Beach – the 8th longest beach in the world (30 mi / 48 km). It is located in Washington, the United States.
- Stockton Beach – the 9th longest beach in the world (20 mi / 32 km). It is located in Australia.
- Muizenberg – the 10th longest beach in the world (20 mi / 32 km). It is located in South Africa.

Beach Cusp

Beach cusp is the arc-shaped landform along the shoreline of an ocean, sea, or lake. It is made of various grades of sediment in an arc pattern. There are beach cusps along the Bay of Bengal, the largest bay in the world.

Beach Ridge

A beach ridge is a wave-deposited ridge running parallel to the shoreline of an ocean, sea, or lake. There are beach ridges on the shoreline of Saaremaa, the largest island in Estonia.

Bedrock
Bedrock is the rock at or near the Earth's surface that is solid and relatively unweathered.

Bench
A bench is a shelf-like area of rock with steep slopes above and below. A bench is a narrow terrace. Benches can be of different origins and created by very different geomorphic processes.

Bight
A bight is a large bay. A bight is shallower than a sound.

Large bights in the world:

- Bay of Campeche in the North Atlantic Ocean
- Bight of Benin in the North Atlantic Ocean
- Bight of Bonny in the North Atlantic Ocean
- Georgia Bight in the North Atlantic Ocean
- German Bight in the North Atlantic Ocean
- Great Australian Bight in the Indian Ocean
- McKenzie Bight in the Pacific Ocean
- Mecklenburg Bight in the North Atlantic Ocean
- Mid-Atlantic Bight in the North Atlantic Ocean
- New York Bight in the North Atlantic Ocean
- North Taranaki Bight in the Pacific Ocean
- Portland Bight in the North Atlantic Ocean
- Robson Bight in the Pacific Ocean
- Southern Bight in the North Atlantic Ocean
- Southern California Bight in the Pacific Ocean
- South Taranaki Bight in the Pacific Ocean
- Trinity Bight in the North Atlantic Ocean

Bill
A bill is a peninsula of land jutting out into the sea. The Portland Bill is located in the United Kingdom.

Biome
A biome is a group of regions with similar climatic conditions. Biomes are sorted differently depending on the system used. Most common types of biomes describe the climate of a country.

Walter System:

- Equatorial – some rain and milder seasons.

- Tropical – seasons are split between a rainy summer and a cooler and dry winter.
- Subtropical – normal seasons, not particularly wet or dry.
- Mediterranean – rainy winter season and dry summer season.
- Warm temperate – rainy summer season and a frosty winter season.
- Nemoral – moderate seasons with a very cold winter season.
- Continental – very dry with hot summers and cold winters.
- Boreal – colder climate with cool summers and long winters.
- Polar – very cold, cool short summer season with a long and cold winter season.

WWF system is used to classify areas by their habitat type:

- Tropical moist forests – broadleaf forest in an area with lots of rain.
- Tropical and subtropical dry broadleaf forest – broadleaf forest in tropical and subtropical latitudes. The area has dry seasons.
- Tropical and subtropical coniferous forests – coniferous forest in tropical and subtropical latitudes. Area is semi-humid.
- Mixed forest – a forest with different types of trees and shrubs. Area is in a temperate climate.
- Temperate coniferous forest – coniferous forest in a temperate area.
- Taiga – coniferous forest in subartic and other drier areas.
- Tropical and subtropical grasslands, savannas, and shrublands – occurs in semiarid or semi humid areas. Consists of grasslands and contains some trees in savannas and shrubs in shrubland.
- Flooded grasslands and savannas – occurs in temperate areas. These grasslands are flooded seasonally.
- Montane grasslands and shrublands – grasslands that are in higher altitudes.
- Tundra – arctic area with cold temperatures and drier. Small patches of grass, moss, lichen, and some shrubs.
- Sclerophyll – small leaved shrubs in a usually drier climate.
- Desert – minimal amount of moisture. Not much vegetation present, if any.
- Mangrove – smaller trees and shrubs in a saline environment, mostly around coastal areas.

Biosphere
The biosphere is the section of Earth where life exists. For Earth, the biosphere contains the ocean floor all the way to tall mountains, as long as life exists at that certain region. The biosphere overlaps with almost all other spheres of Earth.

Blowout Depression
Blowout depressions are sandy depressions in a sand dune ecosystem caused by the removal of sediments by wind. There are deep blowout depressions in the Holy Cross Mountains, Poland.

Blowhole

A blowhole is formed as the sea caves grow landwards and upwards into vertical shafts and expose themselves towards the surface, resulting in quite spectacular blasts of water from the top of the blowhole.

Blowhole examples:

- Alofaaga Blowholes on the Savai'i Island in Samoa
- Hummanaya in Sri Lanka
- Kiama Blowhole in Australia
- Mapu a Vaea on the island of Tongatapu in Tonga

Braided Stream

A braided stream is a shallow stream channel that is subdivided into a number of continually shifting smaller channels that are separated by bar deposits or aits. Extensive braided river systems are found in Alaska of the United States, Canada, New Zealand's South Island, and the Himalayas.

Butte

A butte is a conspicuous isolated hill with steep, often vertical sides and a small, relatively flat top. A butte's top is narrower than its height. It is smaller than a mesa, plateau, or table.

Butte examples in the United States:

- Bear Butte in South Dakota
- Black Butte in Oregon
- Crested Butte in Colorado
- Courthouse Rock in Nebraska
- Elephant Butte in New Mexico
- Merrick's in Monument Valley of Utah
- Scotts Bluff National Monument in Nebraska
- Sutter Buttes in California

Caldera

A caldera is the low rim of a volcano formed when a large volcano collapses into itself after a large eruption.

Largest calderas by size in the world:

- Lake Toba Caldera in Indonesia (62 mi / 100 km x 22 mi / 35 km)
- La Garita in Colorado, the United States (47 mi / 75 km x 22 mi / 35 km)
- Yellowstone Caldera in Wyoming, the United States (45 mi / 72 km x 34 mi / 55 km)

- La Pacana Caldera in Chile (43 mi / 70 km x 22 mi / 35 km)
- Emory Caldera in New Mexico, the United States (34 mi / 55 km x 16 mi / 25 km)
- Pastos Grandes Caldera in Bolivia (31 mi / 50 km x 25 mi / 40 km)
- Lake Taupo Caldera in New Zealand (29 mi / 46 km x 21 mi / 33 km)
- Awasa Caldera in Ethiopia (25 mi / 40 km x 19 mi / 30 km)
- Maroa Caldera in New Zealand (25 mi / 40 km x 19 mi / 30 km)
- Bursum Caldera in New Mexico, the United States (25 mi / 40 km x 19 mi / 30 km)
- Kari Kari Caldera in Bolivia (25 mi / 40 km x 16 mi / 25 km)
- Cerro Galan Caldera in Argentina (25 mi / 40 km x 15 mi / 24 km)
- Socorro Caldera in New Mexico, the United States (22 mi / 35 km x 16 mi / 25 km)
- Longridge Caldera in Oregon, the United States (21 mi / 33 km wide)
- Long Valley Caldera in California, the United States (20 mi / 32 km x 11 mi / 18 km)
- Timber Mountain Caldera in Nevada, the United States (19 mi / 30 km x 16 mi / 25 km)
- Mount Tondano Caldera in Indonesia (19 mi / 30 km x 12 mi / 20 km)
- Chinati Mountains Caldera in Texas, the United States (19 mi / 30 km x 12 mi / 20 km)

Calving

Calving is the loss of glacier mass when ice breaks off into a large water body like an ocean or a lake. The Calving of glaciers usually results in large numbers of icebergs. The Calving of Greenland's glaciers produce 12,000 to 15,000 icebergs each year.

Canyon

A canyon is a steep-sided valley where depth is considerably greater than width, often carved by a river. A canyon is also called a gorge.

Deepest canyons in the world:

- Yarlung Zangbo Grand Canyon – the deepest canyon (from the bottom to the top of the adjacent plateau: 19,715 ft / 6,009 m) in the world, and also the longest canyon (314 mi / 505 km). It is located in China.
- Cotahuasi Canyon – the 2nd deepest canyon in the world (11,598 ft / 3,535 m). It is located in Peru.
- Colca Canyon – the 2nd deepest canyon in Peru (10,499 ft / 3,200 m).
- Kali Gandaki Gorge – the deepest canyon from the highest peak to the lowest river surface (22,310 ft / 6,800 m). It is located in Nepal.
- Hells Canyon – the deepest canyon in the United States (7,993 ft / 2,436 m). It is located in Oregon and Idaho.
- Grand Canyon – the famous canyon located in Arizona, the United States (length: 277 mi / 446 km, depth: 5,699 ft / 1,737 m).
- Copper Canyon in Mexico – includes 6 canyons, large portions are deeper than the Grand Canyon.

Cape

A cape is a point or extension of land jutting out into water as a peninsula or as a projecting point.

Notable capes in Africa:

- Cape of Good Hope in South Africa
- Cape Agulhas in South Africa
- Cape Juby in Morocco
- Cape Guardafui in Somalia
- Cap-Vert in Senegal
- Cape Blanc in Mauritania
- Ras Kasar in Eritrea and Sudan

Notable capes in Europe:

- Cape of Gjuhëz in Albania
- Cape of Rodon in Albania
- Cabo da Roca in Portugal
- Cabo de São Vicente in Portugal
- Cape Arkona in Germany
- Cape Finisterre in Spain
- North Cape in Norway
- Cape Wrath in the United Kingdom
- Cape Cornwall in the United Kingdom
- Cap Gris Nez in France
- Pointe du Razin in France
- Cape Tainaron in Greece
- Cape Emine in Bulgaria
- Cape Kaliakra in Bulgaria
- Cape Greco in Cyprus

Notable capes in Asia:

- Cape Comorin in India
- Cape Engano in Philippines
- Cape Dezhnev in Russia

Notable capes in North America:

- Cape Fear in North Carolina, the United States
- Cape Hatteras in North Carolina, the United States

- Cape Lookout in North Carolina, the United States
- Cape Canaveral in Florida, the United States
- Cape Coral in Florida, the United States
- Cape Charles in Virginia, the United States
- Cape Henry in Virginia, the United States
- Cape Cod in Massachusetts, the United States
- Cape Flattery in Washington, the United States
- Cape May in New Jersey, the United States
- Cape Prince of Wales in Alaska, the United States
- Cape Breton Island in Canada
- Cape Chidley in Canada
- Cape Columbia in Canada
- Cape Spear in Canada
- Cape Farewell in Greenland
- Cabo San Lucas in Mexico

Notable capes in South America:

- Cape Froward in Chile
- Cape Horn in Chile
- Cape Virgenes in Argentina

Notable capes in Oceania

- Cape Egmont in New Zealand
- Cape Foulwind in New Zealand
- Cape Kidnappers in New Zealand
- Cape Reinga in New Zealand
- East Cape in New Zealand
- North Cape in New Zealand
- Cape Leeuwin in Australia
- Cape York in Australia
- South East Cape in Australia

Cave

A cave or cavern is a natural underground space large enough for a human to enter.

Largest caves by size in the world:

- Sarawak Chamber in Gua Nasib Bagus (Good Luck Cave) on the island of Borneo, Malaysia (1,751,288 sq ft / 162,700 m^2)
- Miaos Room in China (1,619,969 sq ft / 150,500 m^2)
- Tlamanictli (TZ1) in Mexico (1,345,489 sq ft / 125,000 m^2)

- Xiniu (Rhino) Chamber in China (861,113 sq ft / 80,000 m^2)
- Torca del Carlista in Spain (824,731 sq ft / 76,620 m^2)
- Unnamed cave in Laos (753,474 sq ft / 70,000 m^2)
- Sistema TZ2-TZ7 in Mexico (645,835 sq ft / 60,000 m^2)
- Sala Gigantilo in Romania (641,604 sq ft / 59,607 m^2)
- Majlis al Jinn in Oman (624,307 sq ft / 58,000 m^2)
- Api Chamber in Whiterock Cave, Malaysia (624,307 sq ft / 58,000 m^2)

Longest caves by total length in the world:

- Mammoth Cave System in Mammoth Cave National Park in Kentucky, the United States (390 mi / 628 km)
- Jewel Cave in Jewel Cave National Monument in South Dakota, the United States (150 mi / 242 km)
- Optymistychna Cave in Ukraine (144 mi / 232 km)
- Wind Cave in Wind Cave National Park in South Dakota, the United States (136 mi / 218 km)
- Sistema Sac Actun in Mexico (135 mi / 217 km, the longest underwater cave)
- Lechuguilla Cave in Carlsbad Caverns National Park in New Mexico, the United States (130 mi / 209 km)
- Hölloch Cave in Switzerland (122 mi / 196 km)
- Fisher Ridge Cave System in Kentucky, the United States (114 mi / 184 km)
- Sistema Ox Bel Ha in Mexico (113 mi / 182 km)
- Gua Air Jernih (Clearwater Cave) in Gunung Mulu National Park on the island of Borneo, Malaysia (109 mi / 176 km, the largest cave by volume: 1,071,713,260 cu ft / 30,347,540 m^3)

Deepest caves in the world:

- Krubera Cave (also called Voronja Cave) in Georgia (7,188 ft / 2,191 m)
- Illyuzia-Mezhonnogo-Snezhnaya Cave in Georgia (5,751 ft / 1,753 m)
- Lamprechtsofen Vogelschacht Weg Schacht in Austria (5,354 ft / 1,632 m)
- Gouffre Mirolda in France (5,335 ft / 1,626 m)
- Reseau Jean Bernard in France (5,256 ft / 1,602 m)
- Cerro del Cuevón in Spain (5,213 ft / 1,589 m)
- Sarma in Georgia (5,062 ft / 1,543 m)
- Shakta Vjacheslav Pantjukhina in Georgia (4,948 ft / 1,508 m)
- Sima de la Cornisa in Spain (4,944 ft / 1,507 m)
- Cehi 2 in Slovenia (4,928 ft / 1,502 m)

Channel

A channel is the physical confine of a river, slough or ocean strait consisting of a bed and banks. It is a natural or human-made deeper course through a reef, sand bar, bay, or any shallow body of water. The Vivari Channel connects Lake Butrint in Albania and the Straits of Corfu.

Cirque

A cirque is an uneven valley head. It is formed by glacial erosion at the head of the valley. The slope of the cirque gets steep then starts to slope upwards. If there is a water source, the cirque will be filled to form a small lake, usually called a tarn.

Notable cirque in Australia:

- Blue Lake Cirque in Australia

Notable cirques in Asia:

- Chandra Taal in India
- Cirque Valley in Pakistan
- Western Cwm in Nepal

Notable cirques in Europe:

- Circo de Gredos in Spain
- Cirque de Gavarnie in France
- Cirque d'Estaubé in France
- Cirque du Fer à Cheval in France
- Coire an t-Sneachda in the United Kingdom
- Śnieżne Kotły in Poland

Notable cirques in North America:

- Cirque of the Towers in Wyoming, the United States
- Iceberg Cirque in Montana, the United States
- Summit Lake Cirque in Colorado, the United States
- Great Basin in Maine, the United States
- Great Gulf in New Hampshire, the United States
- Tuckerman Ravine in New Hampshire, the United States

Cliff

A cliff is a significantly vertical, or near vertical, rock exposure. Cliffs are usually formed by rock that is resistant to erosion and weathering. Sedimentary rocks such as sandstone, limestone, chalk, and dolomite are most likely to form cliffs. Igneous rocks, such as granite and basalt can also often form cliffs.

There is ambiguity about whether a given slope is a cliff or not, and also about how much of a certain slope to count as a cliff.

Tallest cliffs by prominence in Asia:

- Nanga Parbat in Pakistan (15,000 ft / 4,600 m)
- Shispare Sar's southwest face in Pakistan (10,500 ft / 3,200 m)
- Ultar Sar's southwest face in Pakistan (9,800 ft / 3,000 m)
- Lhotse's south face in Nepal (8,500 ft / 2,600 m)
- Spantik's northwest face in Pakistan (6,560 ft / 2,000 m)
- Great Trango Tower's east face in Pakistan (4,400 ft / 1,340 m, near vertical)
- Amin Brakk's southeast face in Pakistan (4,000 ft / 1,200 m, near vertical)

Tallest cliffs by prominence in Europe:

- Troll Wall in Norway (3,600 ft / 1,100 m)
- Mięguszowiecki Szczyt's north face in Poland (3,400 ft / 1,043 m above Morskie Oko Lake)
- Kjerag in Norway (3,200 ft / 984 m)
- Mały Kieżmarski Szczyt's north face in Slovakia (3,000 ft / 900 m)
- Hornelen in Norway (2,800 ft / 860 m above Frøysjøen)
- Giewont's north face in Poland (2,800 ft / 852 m)
- Cape Enniberg in Faroe Islands of Denmark (2,500 ft / 750 m above North Atlantic Ocean)

Tallest cliffs by prominence in North America:

- Ketil's west face in Greenland of Denmark (4,600 ft / 1,400 m)
- Mount Thor's west face in Canada (4,500 ft / 1,370 m)
- Polar Sun Spire's north face in Canada (4,260 ft / 1,300 m)
- Mount Siyeh's north face of Glacier National Park in Montana, the United States (4,170 ft / 1,270 m)
- Mount Asgard in Canada (4,000 ft / 1,200 m)
- North Twin Peak's north face in Canada (4,000 ft / 1,200 m)
- El Capitan of Yosemite Valley in California, the United States (3,000 ft / 900 m)
- Painted Wall of Black Canyon of the Gunnison National Park in Colorado, the United States (2,250 ft / 685 m)
- Half Dome's northwest face of Yosemite Valley in California, the United States (2,000 ft / 610 m)
- Notch Peak's west face of the House Range in Utah, the United States (2,200 ft / 670 m)
- West Temple's east face in Zion National Park in Utah, the United States (2,200 ft / 670 m, the tallest sandstone cliff in the world)
- Big Sandy Mountain's east face buttress of Wind River Range in Wyoming, the United States (1,800 ft / 550 m)
- Warbonnet Peak's northeast face of Wind River Range in Wyoming, the United

- States (1,550 ft / 470 m)
- East Temple Peak's north face of Wind River Range in Wyoming, the United States (1,480 ft / 450 m)
- Lost Temple Spire of Wind River Range in Wyoming, the United States (1,400 ft / 430 m)
- Shiprock in New Mexico, the United States (1,300 ft / 400 m)
- Longs Peak Diamond of Rocky Mountain National Park in Colorado, the United States (1,300 ft / 400 m)
- Temple Peak's east face of Wind River Range in Wyoming, the United States (1,300 ft / 400 m)
- Doublet Peak's southwest face of Wind River Range in Wyoming, the United States (1,200 ft / 370 m)
- Pingora's southeast face of Wind River Range in Wyoming, the United States (1,180 ft / 360 m)
- Royal Gorge cliffs in Colorado, the United States (1,150 ft / 350 m)
- Uncompahgre Peak's northeast face of San Juan Range in Colorado, the United States (900 ft / 275 m)
- Devil's Tower in Wyoming, the United States (640 ft / 195 m)

Tallest cliffs by prominence in South America:

- Autana Tepui in Venezuela (4,260 ft / 1,300 m)
- Cerro Chalten in Argentina and Chile (4,000 ft / 1,200 m)
- Auyan Tepui in Venezuela, (3,280 ft / 1,000 m)
- Torres del Paine in Chile (3,000 ft / 900 m)
- Pared de Gocta in Peru (2,530 ft / 771 m)
- Fortaleza canyon in Brazil (2,360 ft / 720 m)
- Itaimbezinho canyon in Brazil (2,300 ft / 700 m)

Tallest cliffs by prominence in Africa:

- Mount Meru of Caldera Cliffs in Tanzania (4,900 ft / 1,500 m)
- Kogelberg in South Africa (4,229 ft / 1,289 m above Atlantic Ocean)
- Klein Winterhoek in South Africa (4,000 ft / 1,220 m)
- Drakensberg Amphitheatre in South Africa (3,900 ft / 1,200 m)
- Table Mountain in South Africa (3,563 ft / 1,086 m above Atlantic Ocean)
- Fountain Peak in South Africa (3,480 ft / 1,060 m above Atlantic Ocean)
- Risco de Faneque of Canary Islands in Spain (3,369 ft / 1,027 m above Atlantic Ocean)
- Blinkwater Peak in South Africa (3,245 ft / 989 m above Atlantic Ocean)

Tallest cliffs by prominence in Oceania:

- Mitre Peak in New Zealand (5,522 ft / 1,683 m above Milford Sound)
- The Lion in New Zealand (4,272 ft / 1,302 m above Milford Sound)

- The Elephant in New Zealand (3,871 ft / 1,180 m into Milford Sound)
- Kalaupapa in Hawaii, the United States (3,314 ft / 1,010 m above Pacific Ocean)
- Ball's Pyramid in Australia (1,706 ft / 562 m above Pacific Ocean)

Climate

Climate is the generalization of a region's atmosphere, humidity, pressure, and weather over the years. Climate can be classified in different ways. The Köppen classification sorts by the amount of precipitation in that area: tropical, dry, mild mid-latitude, cold mid-latitude, and tundra.

Climate is one of the factors that define a location's biome, as its living conditions are greatly affected by weather.

Cloud

A cloud is a visible mass of condensed water droplets or ice crystals, depending on the temperature of its location. Clouds are typically classified by their shape and their location in the sky.

High altitude cloud types:

- Cirrus – occurs in the upper level of the troposphere in a thin curved shape. Usually made up of ice crystals because of its high elevation. Cirrus clouds can mean an approaching storm with fair weather afterwards.
- Cirrocumulus – occurs in high elevation when moisture hardens into ice crystals. Cirrocumulus clouds look like a series of small puffs.
- Cirrostratus – a continuous sheet of cloud at a high altitude, made up of ice crystals. Can be preceding rain or snow.

Mid-altitude cloud types:

- Altocumulus – a mid-elevation cloud that contains a mass of globular rolls in a layer or patch. Often brings in precipitation.
- Altostratus – a translucent layer of cloud in mid-high elevation. Often is responsible for light precipitation.

Low altitude cloud types:

- Stratocumulus – similar to an altocumulus cloud except at lower altitudes and bigger.
- Stratus – a fog-like cloud but not on the ground.

Multiple layer cloud types:

- Cumulus – puffy clouds with flat bases and domed tops. Can be very large and

multilayered.
- Nimbostratus – a multilayered grey cloud. It is usually developed from altostratus clouds.
- Cumulonimbus – large tall storm clouds. Cumulonimbus clouds develop from towering cumulus clouds until it becomes full sized. When it starts storming, the clouds slowly dissipate from bottom up.

Clouds above the troposphere (very high):

- Polar stratospheric – forms 9 mi – 15 mi (15 km – 24 km) above the surface. Usually occurs during winter when there is most condensation and will look somewhat like a cirrus cloud.
- Polar mesospheric – clouds that form over polar areas. They occur mostly in the summer (when polar areas are colder) at 50 mi – 53 mi (80 km – 85 km) above the surface. Polar mesospheric are night clouds that have ragged edges, and has a similar shape to a cirrus cloud.

Coastal Plain

A coastal plain is an area of flat, low-lying land adjacent to a seacoast and separated from the interior by other features. There are the Gulf Coastal Plain, the Atlantic Coastal Plain, the Lower Coastal Plain, the Upper Costal Pain, and the Arctic Coastal Plain in the United States.

Cold Seep

A cold seep is an area of the ocean floor where hydrogen sulfide, methane and other hydrocarbon-rich fluid seepage occurs, often in the form of a brine pool. Cold seeps constitute a biome supporting several endemic species. A cold seep is also called a cold vent.

Continental Crust

The continental crust is a layer of igneous, sedimentary, and metamorphic rocks which form the continents and the areas of shallow seabed close to their shores, known as continental shelves. The thickness of the continental crust varies between 12 mi – 47 mi (20 km – 75 km). About 40% of the Earth's surface is underlain by continental crust.

Continental Divide

A continental divide is an elevated area that occurs on a continent that divides continental scale drainage basins.

Major continental divides in the world:

- Continental Divide of the Americas (also called the Great Divide) – follows the Rocky mountains, Sierra Madre Occidental, and Andes from Canada through the

United States, Mexico, all the way to the tip of South America, separating the watersheds into the Pacific Ocean from the Atlantic Ocean/the Arctic Ocean.
- Laurentian Divide (also called the Northern Divide) – from eastern Canada, to the United States, and then to the Rocky Mountains, separating the watersheds into the Atlantic Ocean from the Hudson Bay/the Arctic Ocean.
- Saint Lawrence River Divide – follows the Saint Lawrence River in Canada and the United States, separating the watersheds into the Great Lakes from the Atlantic Ocean.
- Eastern Continental Divide – follows the Appalachian Mountains from the Twin Tiers of New York to Florida, separating the watersheds into the Gulf of Mexico from the Atlantic Ocean.
- Arctic Divide – from Canada to the United States, separating the watersheds into the Arctic Ocean from the Hudson Bay.
- Great Dividing Range – located in Australia, separating the watersheds into the Pacific Ocean from the Southern Ocean.
- Tibetan Plateau / Himalaya Mountains – separating the watersheds into the Indian Ocean from the Pacific Ocean.
- Himachal Pradesh in India / Indus-Ganges Plains – separating the watersheds into the Arabian Sea from the Bay of Bengal.
- Atlantic and Mediterranean Divide in Europe – separating the watersheds into the Atlantic Ocean from the Mediterranean Sea.
- Lake Baikal in Russia / Yenisei-Lena Rivers – separating the watersheds into the Kara Sea from the Laptev Sea.
- Perm Krai in Russia / Urals Mountains / Volga-Pechora-Ob Rivers – separating the watersheds into the Caspian Sea from the Arctic Sea.
- Don-Volga Rivers – separating the watersheds into the Black Sea from the Caspian Sea.
- Lunghin Pass in Alps / Rhine-Danube-Po Rivers – separating the watersheds into the North Sea, the Black Sea, and the Adriatic Sea.
- Nile and Congo Divide – passes through the area of the African Great Lakes, separating the watersheds of the Nile River and the Congo River.

Continental Drift
Continental drift is the theory that the Earth's surface consists of tectonic plates that move the Earth's continents from each other. The plates usually move by the movement along fault lines, which can often cause earthquakes. Continental drift is most known for the fact that the continents used to be all together in a super continent known as Pangaea.

Continental Margin
The continental margin is the zone of the ocean floor that separates the thick continental crust from the thin oceanic crust. From inside to outside, the continental margin includes the continental shelf, the continental slope, and the continental rise. Continental margins constitute about 28% of the oceanic area.

Continental Rise
The continental rise is the transition area from the continental crust to the oceanic crust. It is located within the outer part of the continental margin.

Continental Shelf
The continental shelf is the extended perimeter of each continent and associated coastal plain. It is the underwater part of the continental crust. It is located within the inner part of the continental margin.

Continental Slope
The continental slope is the steep portion of continental margin found between the continental shelf and continental rise.

Coral Reef
A coral reef is a type of reef caused by a secretion of creatures called coral.

There are three main types of coral reefs:

- Fringing reef – a coral reef that somehow connects with land. It can also be slightly separated by a lagoon or other smaller body of water.
- Barrier reef – a coral reef that is detached from land. There is a sizable amount of water in between the reef and shore.
- Atoll reef – a coral reef that is round, creating an atoll and a central lagoon in the center.

Largest coral reefs in the world:

- Great Barrier Reef – the largest coral reef in the world, located northeast of Australia.
- Red Sea Coral Reef – the 2nd largest coral reef in the world, located in the Red Sea.
- New Caledonia Barrier Reef – the 3rd largest coral reef in the world, located off the coast of New Caledonia.
- Mesoamerican Barrier Reef – the 4th largest coral reef in the world, located off the coast of Belize.
- Florida Reef – the 5th largest coral reef in the world located off Florida, the United States.
- Andros Reef – the 6th largest coral reef in the world, located near the Bahamas.
- Saya Del Malha – the 7th largest coral reef in the world, located in the Indian Ocean.
- Great Chagos Bank – the 8th largest coral reef in the world, located off the Maldives.
- Reed Bank – the 9th largest coral reef in the world, located off the coast of the Philippines.
- Zongsha Islands – the 10th largest coral reef in the world, located off the coast of China.

Cove

A cove is a small type of bay, usually with narrow, restricted entrances.

Cove examples:

- Lulworth Cove in the United Kingdom
- McWay Cove in the Julia Pfeiffer Burns State Park of California, the United States
- Astwood Cove in Bermuda
- Stair Hole in the United Kingdom

Crater Lake

A crater lake is a lake that forms in a volcanic crater, or in an impact crater caused by a meteorite.

Notable volcanic crater lakes in the world:

- Lagoa das Sete Cidades – a twin-lake in a crater on Azores, Portugal. It is an archipelago of nine volcanic islands in the North Atlantic Ocean.
- Lagoa do Fogo – located in the Agua de Pau stratovolcano on Azores, Portugal.
- Laacher See – a potentially active volcano in the Eifel mountain range, Germany.
- Blue Lake – one of four crater lakes on Mount Gambier, Australia.
- Lake Wisdom – located in Papua New Guinea. Within Lake Wisdom lies a volcanic island named Long Island.
- Lake of Albano – a small lake in the Alban Hills, Italy.
- Lake Nemi – a small lake with sunken Roman ships in Italy.
- Lake Avernus – considered as the entrance to Hades, Italy.
- Lake Bolsena – formed by the collapse of a caldera of the Vulsini volcanic complex in Italy.
- Lake Vico – one of the highest major lakes of Italy.
- Lake Bracciano – one of the major lakes of Italy.
- Lago de Amatitlan – the 4th largest water body in Guatemala.
- Laguna de Calderas – located to the south of Lake Amatitlan in Guatemala.
- Lake Ipala – located at the bottom of the Ipala volcano crater in Guatemala.
- Lago de Atitlan – a large endorheic lake in Guatemala.
- Laguna de Ayarza – a caldera that was created some 20,000 years ago by a catastrophic eruption that destroyed a twinned volcano and blanketed the entire region with a layer of pumice in Guatemala.
- Laguna Chicabal – a lake sacred to the Mam Mayan people in Guatemala.
- Lago de Coatepeque – one of the largest lakes in El Salvador, where there is the island of Teopan, a Mayan site.
- Laguna Verde – located near Apaneca, the highest elevated village in El Salvador.
- Lago De Ilopango – the 2nd largest lake in El Salvador.

- Cuicocha – contains four dacitic lava domes which form two steep forested islands: Yerovi and Teodoro Wolf in Ecuador.
- Heaven Lake – on the top of the Paektu-san on the border of North Korea and China.
- Ijen – a turquoise-colored acid crater lake in Indonesia.
- Lake Toba – the largest volcanic crater lake in Indonesia.
- Segara Anak – located in the Mount Rinjani on the island of Lombok, Indonesia.
- Kelut – known for large explosive eruptions in Indonesia.
- Lago Los Espinos – located in the middle of Mexico.
- Diego de la Haya – located in Irazú Volcano, the highest active volcano in Costa Rica.
- Mount Katmai – formed during the Novarupta eruption of 1912 in Alaska, the United States.
- Green Lake – located in the center of the Kapoho Crater on the Big Island in Hawaii, the United States.
- Yellowstone Lake – the largest body of water in Yellowstone National Park in Wyoming, the United States.
- Crater Lake – located in the caldera of Mount Mazama in Oregon, the United States.
- Medicine Lake – located in the summit area of the Medicine Lake Volcano in California, the United States.
- Newberry Volcano – a large potentially active shield volcano in Oregon, the United States.
- The crater lake in Ojos del Salado – the highest lake of any kind in the world. It is located in Argentina and Chile.
- Laguna del Maule – located in the Andes, Chile.
- Rano Kau – an extinct volcano, located in Rapa Nui National Park, Chile.
- Rano Raraku – located in Rapa Nui National Park, Chile. It is formed of consolidated volcanic ash.
- Kerið – located in Iceland.
- Eyjafjallajökull – located in Iceland.
- Kurile Lake – located in the Southern Kamchatka Wildlife Refuge, Russia.
- Nazko Cone – a small tree-covered cone in Canada.
- Nemrut – a dormant volcano in Turkey.
- Lake Sfânta Ana – the only crater lake in Romania.
- Lake Nyos – located in Cameroon. The eruption suffocated 1,700 people and 3,500 livestock on August 21st, 1986.
- Lake Pinatubo – an active stratovolcano, located in Mount Pinatubo, Philippines.
- Taal Lake – located in the Philippines. It is formed by very large eruptions between 500,000 and 100,000 years ago.
- Mount Ruapehu – located in Tongariro National Park, New Zealand.
- Lake Taupo – the largest lake in New Zealand.
- Lake Shikotsu – located in Shikotsu-Toya National Park, Japan.

- Towada – the 12th largest lake in Japan.
- Mashu – located in Akan National Park on the island of Hokkaido, Japan. It is the clearest lake in the world.
- Tazawa – the deepest lake in Japan.
- Soufrière – an active volcano in Saint Vincent (island), Saint Vincent and the Grenadines.
- Lake Wenchi – an extinct volcano in Ethiopia.
- White Deer Lake – in Hallasan National Park, South Korea.

Notable meteor crater lakes in the world:

- Lonar Crater Lake – a salt lake in India.
- Lake Manicouagan – a reservoir within the remnant of an ancient eroded impact crater in Canada.
- Lake Kaali – a group of 9 meteorite craters in Estonia.
- Lake Siljan – the 6th largest lake in Sweden.
- Lake Dellen – the 18th largest lake in Sweden. It consists of two lakes, Northern Dellen and Southern Dellen, which are connected by a short channel.

Crevasse
A crevasse has two meanings:

- An opening on a levee that allows for the drainage of water from the floodplain to a stream channel
- A deep crack in an ice sheet or glacier

Crevice
A crevice is a deep crack in rock.

Cuesta
A cuesta is an asymmetric ridge characterized by a short, steep escarpment on one side, and a long, gentle slope on the other side. Cuestas are typically made out of sedimentary layers, with the layers more resistant to erosion forming the higher edges and the less resistant dug out as depressions.

Cuspate Foreland
A cuspate foreland is a triangular accumulation of sand and other particles located along the coastline. The cuspate foreland is formed by the joining of two spits. Cuspate forelands occur in Dungeness, the United Kingdom, and Cape Canaveral in Florida, the United States.

Delta
A delta is a large deposit of alluvial sediment located at the mouth of a river where a river flows into an ocean, sea, estuary, lake, reservoir, flat arid area, or another river. Deltas tend

to exist at the end of any sizable river. The exception would be the Amazon River, which is the 2nd longest river in the world but does not have a delta. The Ganges Delta at the mouth of the Brahmaputra River in Bangladesh/India is the largest delta in the world by water flow.

Other notable deltas in the world:

- Nile River Delta – located at the end of the Nile River in northern Egypt into the Mediterranean Sea. It is the longest river delta in the world.
- Niger River Delta – located at the end of the Niger River in southwestern Nigeria into the Atlantic Ocean.
- Tigris-Euphrates Delta – located at the convergence of the Tigris and Euphrates Rivers at the Persian Gulf in southeastern Iraq.
- Rhine River Delta – located at the end of the Rhine River in the Netherlands. The river empties into the North Sea.
- Po River Delta – located at the end of the Po River in Italy. The river empties into the Adriatic Sea.
- Rhone River Delta – located at the end of the Rhone River in France. The river empties into the Mediterranean Sea.
- Danube River Delta – the 2nd largest delta in Europe, located at the mouth of the Danube River in Romania. The river empties into the Black Sea.
- Ebro River Delta – located at the end of the Ebro River in Spain. The river empties into the Mediterranean Sea.
- Volga River Delta – the largest delta in Europe, located at the mouth of the Volga River in Russia. The river empties into the Caspian Sea.
- Lena River Delta – located at the end of the Lena River in Russia. The river empties into the Arctic Ocean. The delta is also a wildlife preserve.
- Indus River Delta – located at the end of the Indus River in Pakistan. The river empties into the Arabian Sea.
- Mahanadi River Delta – located at the end of the Mahanadi River in India. The river empties into the Bay of Bengal.
- Krishna-Godavari Delta – located at the conjunction of the Krishna and Godavari Rivers in India. The rivers empty into the Bay of Bengal.
- Kaveri River Delta – located at the end of the Kaveri River in India. The river empties into the Bay of Bengal.
- Ayeyarwady River Delta – located at the end of the Ayeyarwady and some more minor rivers in Myanmar. The rivers empty into the Andaman Sea.
- Mekong River Delta – located at the mouth of the Mekong River in Vietnam. The river empties into the South China Sea.
- Yellow River Delta – located at the end of the Yellow River in China. The river empties into the Bonhai Sea. The delta is considered to be vital to Chinese civilization.
- Yangtze River Delta – located at the end of the Yangtze River in China. The river empties into the East China Sea. The city of Shanghai lies on the delta.

- Sacramento-San Joaquin Delta – located at the conjunction of the Sacramento River and San Joaquin River in California, the United States. The rivers empty into the Pacific Ocean through the San Francisco Bay.
- Mississippi River Delta – located at the end of the Mississippi River in Louisiana, the United States. The river empties into the Gulf of Mexico. New Orleans lies on the delta.
- Orinoco River Delta – located at the end of the Orinoco River in Venezuela. The river empties into the Atlantic Ocean.
- Parana River Delta – located at the end of the Parana River in Argentina. The river empties into the Atlantic Ocean.

Desert

A desert is a landscape or region that receives an extremely low amount of precipitation, less than 10 in (250 mm) per year. The Gandom Beryan in the Lut Desert, Iran, is the hottest place in the world.

Largest deserts by size in the world:

- Antarctic Desert – the largest desert in the world (5,339,573 sq mi / 13,829,430 km^2), covering the majority of the continent of Antarctica.
- Sahara Desert – the 2nd largest desert in the world (3,320,000 sq mi / 9,100,000 km^2), stretching from the Atlantic Ocean to the Red Sea.
- Arabian Desert – the 3rd largest desert in the world (900,000 sq mi / 2,330,000 km^2), covering the majority of the Arabian Peninsula and stretching towards Iraq.
- Gobi Desert – the 4th largest desert in the world (500,000 sq mi / 1,300,000 km^2), covering part of China and Mongolia.
- Kalahari Desert – the 5th largest desert in the world (360,000 sq mi / 900,000 km^2), covering the majority of Botswana and parts of Namibia and South Africa. It is a semi desert, as there are still some plants for grazing amongst the sand.
- Patagonian Desert – the 6th largest desert in the world (260,000 sq mi / 670,000 km^2), covering part of Argentina and Chile.
- Great Victoria Desert – the 7th largest desert in the world (250,000 sq mi / 647,000 km^2), covering part of the southern part of Australia.
- Syrian Desert – the 8th largest desert in the world (200,000 sq mi / 520,000 km^2), covering areas from Syria to Saudi Arabia. It is somewhat an extension of the Arabian Desert.
- Great Basin Desert – the 9th largest desert in the world (190,000 sq mi / 492,000 km^2), covering the southeastern United States, from Nevada extending to California, Oregon, Idaho, Utah, and Wyoming.

Desert Pavement

A desert pavement is a desert surface that is covered with closely packed, interlocking angular or rounded rock fragments of pebble and cobble. There are desert pavements in the Sahara Desert, the Rub' al-Khali Desert, the Mojave Desert, and the Tirari-Sturt stony desert.

Desert Varnish
Desert varnish is a dark coating found on exposed rock surfaces in arid environments. Desert varnish is also called rock varnish, rock rust, or desert patina. There is desert varnish at the Valley of Fire in Nevada, the United States.

Dissected Plateau
A dissected plateau is a plateau area that has been severely eroded so that the relief, the angle of its incline, is sharper than that of a normal plateau. The Ozark Plateau is a dissected plateau in the central United States.

Drainage Divide
A drainage divide is the line separating neighboring drainage basins. A drainage divide is also called a water divide, divide, or watershed.

Types of drainage divides:

- Continental Divide – a divide in which the waters on each side flow to different oceans.
- Major Drainage Divide – the waters on each side of the divide never meet again, but do flow into the same ocean, such as the divide between the Yellow River and Yangtze Rivers.
- Minor Drainage Divide – the waters on each side of the divide part but eventually join again at a river confluence, such as the divide between the Mississippi River and the Missouri River

Dreikanter
A Dreikanter is a pebble typically having three curved faces shaped by wind-blown sand. Dreikanters are common in desert areas.

Drumlin
A drumlin is a whale shaped hill shaped by glacial activity. Drumlins are usually created when the glacier is receding, so its shape will match the direction that the glacier was going towards. Drumlins can be found in a group, called a drumlin field. The Clew Bay in Ireland is an example of a place that contains many drumlins.

Dry Lake
A dry lake is a temporary riverbed or a remnant of a lake without an inflow. The surface of a dry lake will be dry and hard during the dry season while wet and soft during the rainy season. Sometimes there will be enough rain to form a temporary small lake in the riverbed.

Dune

A dune is a hill of sand formed by the wind. There are five basic types of dunes: crescentic, linear, star, dome, and parabolic. The most common dune type is the crescentic.

Tallest dunes by prominence in the world:

- Cerro Blanco – the tallest dune in the world (3,860 ft / 1,176 m), located in the Sechura Desert of Peru.
- Medanoso Dunev – the 2nd tallest dune in the world (1,805 ft / 550 m), located in the Atacama Desert of Chile.
- Badain Jaran Dunes – the tallest dunes in Asia (1,640 / 500 m), located in the Badain Jaran Desert and the Gobi Desert of China.
- Dunes in the Sahara Desert – the tallest dunes in Africa (1,526 / 465 m), located in the Algerian portion of the Sahara Desert.
- Mount Tempest – the tallest dune in Australia (920 ft / 280 m), located in the Moreton Bay.
- Star Dune – the tallest dune in North America (750 ft / 230 m), located in Great Sand Dunes National Park and Preserve of Colorado, the United States.
- Dune of Pyla – the tallest dune in Europe (345 ft / 105 m), located in the Bay of Arcachon, France.

Earthquake

An earthquake is a sudden release of energy inside the Earth's crust. An earthquake causes shaking by the release of seismic waves. Earthquakes can occur anywhere on the Earth's crust as long as there is sufficient stress, but major ones would usually be limited to earthquake faults. The magnitude of an earthquake can often be determined by the type of fault which causes it. A strike-slip fault tends to create weaker earthquakes than dip-slip faults. The area in the world most susceptible to earthquakes is the Ring of Fire, the areas bordering the Pacific Ocean.

Earthquakes can cause a variety of other natural disasters: landslides, soil liquefaction, tsunami, and floods.

The magnitude of an earthquake is most commonly measured by the Richter Scale. The Richter Scale is a logarithmic scale, where a magnitude 0 earthquake causes a displacement of one micrometer. Every whole number increase would represent an earthquake 10 times larger.

El Niño

El Nino is a phenomenon which causes wet winters in the southwestern United States while causing droughts in southeastern Asia. El Niño is caused by strong winds which cause the water temperature to be colder on the west side of the Pacific Ocean and warmer on the east side of the Pacific Ocean.

Endorheic Basin

An endorheic basin is a closed drainage basin that retains water and allows no outflow to other bodies of water such as rivers or oceans. The Caspian Sea is an endorheic basin.

Eolianite

An eolianite is a sedimentary rock consisting of clastic material which has been deposited by wind. The most extensive deposits of eolianite in the world are located on the southern and western coasts of Australia.

Erosion

Erosion is the process of weathering and transportation of sediment, soil, rock and other particles in the natural environment and depositing them elsewhere. Erosion is caused by forces of wind, water, and/or ice. Approximately 40% of the world's agricultural land is seriously degraded.

Erg

An erg is a large, relatively flat area of desert covered with wind-swept sand with little or no vegetative cover. Erg is also called sand sea or dune sea. There are a lot of ergs in the Saharan Desert region.

Escarpment

An escarpment is a steep slope or long cliff that results from erosion or faulting and separates two relatively level areas of differing elevations.

Notable escarpments in the world:

- Elgeyo Escarpment in the Great Rift Valley
- Drakensberg Escarpment in South Africa
- Great Escarpment in South Africa
- Bandiagara Escarpment in Mali
- Zambezi Escarpment in Zambia
- Scarp of Angola in Angola
- Usas Escarpment in Antarctica
- Vindhyan Escarpment in India
- Darling Scarp in Australia
- Dorrigo Plateau in Australia
- Illawarra Escarpment in Australia
- Nullarbor Escarpment in Australia
- Southern Alps in New Zealand
- Kaimai Escarpment in New Zealand
- Cotswold Escarpment in the United Kingdom

- North Downs in the United Kingdom
- South Downs in the United Kingdom
- Alderley Edge in the United Kingdom
- Edge Hill in the United Kingdom
- Kinver Edge in the United Kingdom
- Lincoln Edge in the United Kingdom
- Wenlock Edge in the United Kingdom
- Côte d'Or and Pays de Bray in France
- Swabian Alb in Germany
- Baltic Klint in Sweden, Estonia, and Russia
- Gotland–Saaremaa Klint in Sweden, Estonia, and Russia
- Victoria Lines in Malta

Esker

An esker is a ridge of sand and gravel. The sand and gravel is usually separated into different layers. An esker is created by glacial activity. Eskers can be hundreds of miles long, and will generally have a similar width throughout. The Thelon Esker in Canada is an example of an esker.

Estuary

Estuary is an enclosed coastal area at the mouth of a river where the freshwater from the river meets with salty ocean water.

Notable estuaries in the United States:

- Albemarle Sound in North Carolina
- Chesapeake Bay in Maryland and Virginia
- Delaware Bay in New Jersey and Delaware
- Great Bay in New Hampshire
- Great Bay in New Jersey
- Laguna Madre in Texas
- Lake Pontchartrain in Louisiana
- Long Island Sound in Connecticut and New York
- Mobile Bay in Alabama
- Narragansett Bay in New England
- New York Harbor in New York
- Puget Sound in Washington
- Pamlico Sound in North Carolina
- San Francisco Bay in California

Notable estuaries elsewhere in the world:

- Amazon River estuary in Brazil

- Golden Horn in Turkey
- Gulf of Saint Lawrence in Canada
- Ob River estuary in Russia
- Rio de la Plata in Argentina and Uruguay
- Shannon Estuary in Ireland
- Humber in the United Kingdom
- Thames Estuary in the United Kingdom

The Gulf of Saint Lawrence is the largest estuary in the world, where the Great Lakes via the Saint Lawrence River flows into the Atlantic Ocean. The Ob River estuary is the longest estuary in the world.

Exhumed River Channel

An exhumed river channel is a ridge of sandstone that remains when the softer flood plain mudstone is eroded away. There are exhumed river channels in the Ruby Ranch Member of the Cretaceous Cedar Mountain Formation southwest of Green River in Utah, the United States.

Fault

A fault is a discontinuity in rock. Faults usually separate different plates of the Earth's crust.

Types of faults:

- Dip-slip fault – a fault that is cut at about a 45 degree angle. One of the plates will hang above the other and they collide.
- Strike-slip fault – a fault that moves sideways across each other.
- Oblique-slip faults – a fault that is a mix of dip-slip and strike-slip faults. The fault can be cut at a 45 degree angle making one fault move over the other but it will also move sideways.
- Listric fault – a fault that is curved.
- Ring fault – a fault that is located in a caldera of a volcano.

The Mid-Atlantic Range, a diverging (plates moving away from each other) fault separating the American and Eurasian plates is an example of a major dip-slip fault fault. San Andreas Fault, fault that runs through California is an example of a major strike-slip fault.

Firn

Firn is a type of snow that survives a full season of ablation. It is older and slightly denser than Névé. With time much of the firn is transformed into glacial ice. Glacier formation can take days to years depending on freeze-thaw factors. The density of firn generally ranges 34 lb/ft³ – 52 lb/ft³ (550 kg/m³ – 830 kg/m³).

Firth

Firth is a long, narrow inlet of the sea in Scotland. A firth would be called fjord if it is in Scandinavia. The Moray Firth is the largest firth in Scotland.

Fjord

A fjord is a long, narrow inlet of the sea with steep sides or cliffs, created in a valley carved by glacial activity. The Scoresby Sund in Greenland is the largest and longest fjord system in the world (size: 14,700 sq mi / 38,000 km^2, length: 217 mi / 350 km). Fjords are a symbol of Norway, which contains some of the longest, deepest, and most beautiful fjords in the world.

Flood Basalt

A flood basalt is the remnant of a giant volcanic eruption or series of eruptions that coats large stretches of land or the ocean floor with basalt lava. Flood basalts have occurred on continental scales in prehistory, creating great plateaus and mountain ranges. A flood basalt is also called a trap basalt.

Major flood basalts in the world:

- Columbia-Snake River flood basalts – a large flood basalt that lies across Washington, Oregon, Idaho, California, and Nevada, the United States. The flood basalt was part of a huge flood basalt that once occupied the entire Pacific Northwest.
- Ethiopian and Yemen traps – also known as the Arabian-Nubian Shield. It covers Israel, Jordan, Egypt, Saudi Arabia, Sudan, Eritrea, Ethiopia, Yemen, and Somalia.
- North Atlantic Volcanic Province – a flood basalt in the North Atlantic Ocean. In ancient times the basalt spread into Greenland and the United Kingdom.
- Deccan Traps – a flood basalt in India.
- Caribbean large igneous province – a flood basalt that created the Caribbean Islands as well as islands in the eastern Pacific Ocean.
- Kerguelen Plateau – a flood basalt in the Southern Indian Ocean.
- Ontong Java–Manihiki–Hikurangi Plateau – a large flood basalt near the Solomon Islands.
- Paraná and Etendeka traps – a flood basalt in Brazil, Angola, and Namibia. The flood basalt was separated when the continent of South America and Africa drifted apart.
- Karoo and Ferrar provinces – a flood basalt that covers part of South Africa and Antarctica, as well as Australia and New Zealand.
- Central Atlantic Magmatic Province – a flood basalt that covers part of the North Atlantic Ocean.
- Siberian Traps – a flood basalt that covers about half of the area of Siberia in Russia.
- Emeishan Traps – a flood basalt that covers part of southwestern China.
- Coppermine River Group – a flood basalt in northern Canada. It is one of the biggest flood basalts in the world. The region also expands into the Mackenzie Large Igneous Province.

- Strand Fiord Formation – a flood basalt in northern Canada.
- Chilcotin Group – a flood basalt in southwestern Canada.
- North Mountain Basalt – a flood basalt in the Nova Scotia region of Canada.

Floodplain

A floodplain is a flat patch of land located next to a stream or river. It is the region next to the river that floods often. While dangerous, many towns and cities are built on the floodplain due to the proximity of fresh water, easy transportation, and the flatness of the land. An example of a vulnerable city on a floodplain is Dhaka, Bangladesh.

Fluvial terrace

A fluvial terrace is an elongated terrace that flanks floodplains. A fluvial terrace is formed when the flow in a river decreases. The floodplain of the river at the old elevation then slowly develops into a fluvial terrace.

Types of fluvial terraces:

- Fill Terrace – made by an influx of alluvium, a type of sediment, into the river valley.
- Strath Terrace – made as the river flows erodes bedrock, making the valley deeper.
- Paired Terrace – having the same elevation on both sides.
- Unpaired Terrace – having a different elevation on each side of the river.

Forest

An area with a cluster of trees, usually with an overstory, an area with tall growing trees, and an understory, shrubs and smaller plans that grow underneath the tree cover.

Types of forests:

- Temperate needleleaf – occurs mainly in the northern part of the northern hemisphere. Soil quality is usually poor.
- Temperate broadforest and mixed – occurs in warmer latitudes. Includes varied types of trees. Temperate broadforest and mixed forests can be found in Japan, China, Chile, Australia, and the United States.
- Tropical moist – occurs in tropical latitudes. The most famous tropical moist forest is the Amazon Rainforest.
- Tropical dry – occurs in tropical latitudes. A tropical dry forest is a tropical forest that suffers from seasonal drought. There are a lot more coniferous trees in tropical dry forests.
- Sparse trees – often located in higher latitudes. Sparse tree forests indicate a forest with openings in the canopy. Sparse tree forests are usually made up of more evergreen trees.

Countries containing the most forested areas: Russia, Brazil, Canada, the United States, and China.

Geyser

A geyser is a spring that expels intermittent discharges of hot water. There are two types of geysers: fountain geysers and cone geysers. Fountain geysers erupt from pools of water, typically in a series of intense, violent, bursts, e.g. Grand Geyser in Yellowstone National Park. Cone geysers erupt from cones or mounds of siliceous sinter, a type of mineral deposit, usually in steady jets, e.g. Old Faithful Geyser in Yellowstone National Park.

Notable geyser fields in the world:

- Yellowstone National Park – the largest geyser locale, containing 300 to 500 geysers, including Old Faithful Geyser, Steamboat Geyser, Grand Geyser, Beehive Geyser, Giantess Geyser, Lion Geyser, Plume Geyser, Aurum Geyser, Castle Geyser, Sawmill Geyser, Oblong Geyser, Giant Geyser, Daisy Geyser, Grotto Geyser, Fan & Mortar Geysers, and Riverside Geyser. It is located in Wyoming, Montana and Idaho, the United States.
- Valley of Geysers – the 2nd largest geyser locale, containing 90 geysers, part of the Kronotsky Nature Reserve in Kamchatka Peninsula. It is located in Russia.
- El Tatio – the 3rd largest geyser locale, containing 80 geysers, in the high valleys on the Andes. It is located in Chile.
- Taupo Volcanic Zone – includes the largest extinct geyser, Waimangu Geyser. It is located on the North Island, New Zealand.
- Iceland – distributed all over the island, but many of the geysers are located in Haukadalur.

Notable geysers in the world:

- Waimangu – the tallest geyser in the world (1,500 ft / 460 m). Waimangu is currently extinct. It is located in New Zealand.
- Steamboat Geyser – the 2nd tallest geyser in the world (390 ft / 120 m). It is located in Yellowstone National Park in Wyoming, Montana and Idaho, the United States.
- Excelsior Geyser – the 3rd tallest geyser in the world (300 ft / 91 m). It is located in Yellowstone National Park in Wyoming, Montana and Idaho, the United States.
- Minquini – the 4th tallest geyser in the world (295 ft / 90 m). Minquini is currently extinct. It is located in New Zealand.
- Giant Geyser – the 5th tallest geyser in the world (250 ft / 76 m). It is located in Yellowstone National Park in Wyoming, Montana and Idaho, the United States.
- Grand Geyser – the 8th tallest geyser in the world (200 ft / 61 m). The Grand Geyser is the tallest geyser whose discharges are predictable. It is located in Yellowstone National Park in Wyoming, Montana and Idaho, the United States.
- Old Faithful Geyser – the 14th tallest geyser in the world (185 ft / 56 m). The Old Faithful Geyser has the most frequent discharges of water. It is located in

Yellowstone National Park in Wyoming, Montana and Idaho, the United States.

Glacier

A glacier is a large persistent body of snow and ice that develops on land. Most glaciers flow along topographic gradients because of their weight and gravity. Glaciers can be found in mountain ranges of every continent. In the tropics, glaciers occur only on high mountains. The Lambert Glacier in Antarctica is the largest glacier in the world (250 mi / 400 km long, 60 mi / 100 km wide, and 8,202 ft / 2,500 m deep).

Types of glaciers:

- Ice sheet / continental glacier – the largest glacial body, covering an area of more than 20,000 sq mi (50,000 km²). The only extant ice sheets are the two that cover most of Antarctica and Greenland.
- Ice shelf – occurs when an ice sheet extend over the sea, and float on the water. Ice shelves surround most of the Antarctic continent.
- Ice cap – a miniature ice sheet, covering less than 20,000 sq mi (50,000 km²). The much smaller mass of ice on Iceland is an ice cap.
- Ice stream – a fast-moving section of an ice sheet. The Antarctic ice sheet has many ice streams flowing outward.
- Ice field – similar to an ice cap without the dome-like form. The ice fields are common in Arctic Canada, Alaska, the Andes in South America, the Himalayas in Asia, and on Antarctica.
- Mountain glacier – develops in high mountainous regions, often flowing out of ice fields and is smaller than an ice field. The largest mountain glaciers are found in Arctic Canada, Alaska, the Andes in South America, the Himalayas in Asia, and on Antarctica.
- Valley glacier – commonly originates from mountain glaciers or ice fields. Valley glaciers spill down valleys, looking much like giant tongues.
- Piedmont glacier – occurs when steep valley glaciers spill into relatively flat plains, where they spread out into bulb-like lobes. The Malaspina Glacier in Alaska, the United States, is the largest piedmont glacier in the world (1,500 sq mi / 3,900 km²).
- Cirque glacier – named for the bowl-like hollows it occupies, which are called cirques. The Pastoruri glacier in Peru is a cirque glacier.
- Hanging glacier / ice apron – clings to steep mountainsides. Hanging glaciers are common in the Alps, where they often cause avalanches due to the steep inclines they occupy.
- Tidewater glacier – a glacier that terminate in the sea. Tidewater glaciers are responsible for calving numerous small icebergs. The Hubbard Glacier is the longest tidewater glacier in Alaska, the United States, and Canada (76 mi / 122 km).

Glacier Cave

A glacier cave is a cave that is formed within a glacier. Glacier caves are usually created when the water melted from the glacier erodes part of the glacier forming a cave-like formation. In areas of volcanic activity, geothermal heat can also create a glacier cave. The Kverkfjöll cave is an example of a glacier cave.

Gulch

A gulch is a deep V-shaped valley formed by erosion. It may contain a small stream or dry creek bed and is usually larger than a gully. The Chili Gulch is a gulch in California, the United States.

Gulf

A Gulf is a large bay that is an arm of an ocean or sea.

Notable gulfs in the Pacific Ocean:

- Gulf of Alaska – bordered by the United States and Canada.
- Gulf of Carpentaria – bordered by Australia, Indonesia and Papua New Guinea.
- Gulf of Tonkin – bordered by Vietnam and China.

Notable gulfs in the Indian Ocean:

- Persian Gulf – bordered by Iran, Iraq, Kuwait, Saudi Arabia, Qatar, Bahrain, United Arab Emirates and Oman.
- Gulf of Aqaba – bordered by Egypt, Israel, Amman, and Saudi Arabia.
- Gulf of Aden – bordered by Yemen and Somali.
- Gulf of Suez – bordered by Egypt.

Notable gulf in the Atlantic Ocean:

- Gulf of Kuşadası – bordered by Turkey and Greece.
- Gulf of Lion – bordered by France and Spain.
- Gulf of Mexico – bordered by the United States, Mexico, and Cuba.
- Gulf of Morbihan – bordered by France.
- Gulf of Odessa – bordered by Ukraine.
- Gulf of Oristano – bordered by Italy.
- Gulf of Bothnia – bordered by Finland and Sweden.
- Gulf of Finland – bordered by Finland, Estonia, and Russia.
- Gulf of Riga – bordered by Latvia and Estonia.
- Gulf of Roses – bordered by Spain.
- Gulf of Saint Lawrence – bordered by Canada.

The Gulf of Mexico is the largest gulf in the world (615,000 sq mi / 1,600,000 km²).

Gully

A gully is a landform created by running water, eroding sharply into soil, typically on a hillside. Artificial gullies were formed during the gold rush in California, the United States and northern Spain.

Headland
Headland is a strip of land, usually of high elevation, that juts seaward from the coastline. The Beachy Head is a headland in the United Kingdom.

Hill
A hill is land that extends above its surrounding areas without a sharp angle. Hills are usually referred as mountains that are less than 1,000 ft – 2,000 ft (305 m – 610 m) above sea level. The Canaval Hill in Oklahoma, the United States, claims to be the tallest hill in the world at 1,999 ft (609 m) above sea level.

Hogback
A hogback is a narrow ridge that consists of steeply inclined rock strata. The Dakota Hogback is a long hogback ridge at the eastern fringe of the Rocky Mountains in the United States.

Hoodoo
A hoodoo is a column of weathered and unusually shaped rock. There are hoodoos in Bryce Canyon National Park, the United States.

Hydrosphere
Hydrosphere is the total mass of all the water on, over, or under a planet's surface. In total, the Earth's hydrosphere covers about 75% of its entire surface, with an average salinity of 3.5%.

Iceberg
An iceberg is a floating piece of ice on water. Icebergs either break off from glaciers or an ice pack. An iceberg's size usually is $8/9^{th}$ underwater, making it much larger than it actually seems on first sight.

Types of icebergs:

- Dome – an iceberg with a rounded top.
- Pinnacle – an iceberg with spire(s) at the top.
- Wedge – an iceberg with a steel slope on one side and a shallower slope on the other.
- Dry dock – an eroded iceberg that forms a channel.
- Blocky – an iceberg with a shape similar to an ice cube.

Inlet

An inlet is a passage by which an enclosed place may be entered. The Howe Sound, near Vancouver, Canada, is a large inlet.

Island

An island is region of sub continental land surrounded by water. Small islands can be known as islets, cays, or keys. Inland islands (rivers and lakes) can be called eyots. There are two main types of islands – continental or oceanic. Continental islands are islands that lie on a continental shelf while oceanic islands do not.

Largest islands by size in the world:

- Greenland – the largest island in the world (822,706 sq mi / 2,130,800 km^2). It is a part of Denmark.
- New Guinea – the 2nd largest island in the world (303,381 sq mi / 785,753 km^2). It is located Indonesia and Papua New Guinea.
- Borneo –the 3rd largest island in the world (288,869 sq mi / 748,168 km^2). It is located in Brunei, Indonesia, and Malaysia.
- Madagascar – the 4th largest island in the world (226,917 sq mi / 587,713 km^2).
- Baffin Island – the 5th largest island in the world (195,928 sq mi / 507,451 km^2). It is located in Canada.
- Sumatra – the 6th largest island in the world (171,069 sq mi / 443,066 km^2). It is located in Indonesia.
- Honshu – the 7th largest island in the world (87,182 sq mi / 225,800 km^2). It is located in Japan.
- Victoria Island – the 8th largest island in the world (83,897 sq mi / 217,291 km^2). It is located in Canada.
- Great Britain – the 9th largest island in the world (80,823 sq mi / 209,331 km^2). It is located in the United Kingdom.
- Ellesmera Island – the 10th largest island in the world (75,767 sq mi / 196,236 km^2). It is located in Canada.

Island Arc

An island arc is tectonically created arc-shaped mountain belt that is partly below sea level. Many of island arcs are composed of volcanoes, but not necessarily composed solely of volcanoes.

Isthmus

An isthmus is a narrow strip of land connecting two larger land areas usually with water bodies on either side.

Notable isthmuses in the world:

- Isthmus of Kra – connects Malay Peninsula and the mainland of Asia, between the

Andaman Sea and the Gulf of Thailand. It is located in Thailand and Myanmar.
- Isthmus of Suez – connects North Africa and Sinai Peninsula, between the Gulf of Aqaba and the Mediterranean Sea. It is located in Egypt.
- Caucasus region – connects Europe and Asia, between the Black Sea and the Caspian Sea. It is located in Armenia, Azerbaijan, Georgia, and Russia.
- Eaglehawk Neck – connects the Tasman Peninsula and the mainland of Tasmania, between the Storm Bay and the Tasman Sea. It is located in Australia.
- Neck in Bruny Island of Tasmania – connects North and South Bruny, between the D'Entrecasteaux Channel and the Storm Bay. It is located in Australia.
- Auckland isthmus – connects the Northland Peninsula and the rest of New Zealand's North Island, between the Tasman Sea and the Pacific Ocean.
- Rongotai Isthmus – connects the Miramar Peninsula and the rest of Wellington, between the Kilbirnie Bay and the Lyall Bay. It is located in New Zealand.
- Isthmus of Corinth – connects the Peloponnese Peninsula and the rest of Greece, between the Gulf of Corinth and the Saronic Gulf.
- Isthmus of Potidea – connects the Kassandra Peninsula and the mainland of Greece, between two parts in the Aegean Sea.
- Isthmus of Catanzaro – connects the two parts of Italy, between the .Tyrrhenian Sea and the Ionian Sea.
- Isthmus of Gibraltar – connects the Rock and the mainland of Spain, between the Bay of Gibraltar and the Alboran Sea. It is located in Gibraltar.
- Isthmus of Perekop – connects the Crimea Peninsula and the mainland of Ukraine, between the Black Sea and the Azov Sea.
- Karelian Isthmus – connects two parts of Russia, between Lake Ladoga and the Gulf of Finland.
- Olonets Isthmus – connects two parts of Russia, between Lake Ladoga and Lake Onega.
- La Coupée Isthmus – connects Great Sark and Little Sark in the Channel Islands, between two bays in the English Channel. It is located in the United Kingdom.
- Forth-Clyde Isthmus – connects two parts of Scotland, between the Firth of Forth and the Firth of Clyde. It is located in the United Kingdom.
- Mavis Grind Isthmus – connects the Northmavine Peninsula and the rest of the island of Shetland Mainland in the Shetland Islands, between the North Sea and the Atlantic Ocean. It is located in the United Kingdom.
- Rhins of Galloway Isthmus – connects two parts of Scotland, between the Loch Ryan and the Luce Bay. It is located in the United Kingdom.
- Bardsey Island Isthmus – connects the Llŷn Peninsula and the rest of the Bardsey Island, between the Cardigan Bay and the Caernarfon Bay. It is located in the United Kingdom.
- Isthmus of Westfjords Peninsula – connects to the Westfjords Peninsula and the mainland of Iceland, between Gilsfjörður and Bitrufjörður
- Isthmus of Austin Travis – connects two parts of Texas, between two parts of Lake Travis. It is located in the United States.
- Madison Isthmus – connects two parts of Wisconsin, between Lake Mendota and

Lake Monona. It is located in the United States.
- Seattle – connects Seattle and the rest of Washington, between the Puget Sound and Lake Washington. It is located in the United States.
- Isthmus of Avalon – connects the Avalon Peninsula and the rest of the island of Newfoundland, between the Gulf Saint Lawrence and the Atlantic Ocean. It is located in Canada.
- Isthmus of Chignecto – connects the Nova Scotia Peninsula and the North America, between the Bay of Fundy and the Northumberland Strait. It is located in Canada.
- Isthmus of Tehuantepec – connects two parts of Mexico, between the Gulf of Mexico and the Pacific Ocean.
- Isthmus of Rivas – connects two parts of Nicaragua, between the Lake Nicaragua and the Pacific Ocean.
- Isthmus of Panama – connects the North America and South America, between the Gulf of Panama and the Caribbean Sea. It is located in Panama.
- Isthmus of Médanos – connects the Paraguaná Peninsula and the rest of Venezuela, between the Gulf of Venezuela and the Caribbean Sea.
- Ofqui Isthmus – connects the Taitao Peninsula and the Chilean mainland, between the Gulf of Penas and the San Rafael Lagoon.
- Istmo Carlos Ameghino – connects the Valdes Peninsula and the Argentina mainland, between two bays, Golfo San José and Golfo Nuevo.
- Isthmus of Falkland Islands – connects Lafonia and the rest of the East Falkland, between two fjords, Choiseul Sound and Brenton Loch-Grantham Sound. It is a part of the United Kingdom.

Kame
A kame is an irregular shaped hill made of sand, gravel, and till. Kames are typically made from glacial activity, from the sediments stacking on a depression made by the glacier. The kame is then shaped by water from the melting glacier. The path of the water will sometimes from a kame delta, a triangle shape similar to a river delta. The Fonthill Kame in Canada is an example of a kame.

Karst
Karst is a type of landscape shaped by the dissolution of a layer or layers of soluble bedrock, usually carbonate rock such as limestone or dolomite. Sinkholes are the most common feature of karst surfaces. Various karst landforms have been found on all continents except Antarctica.

Kettle
A kettle is a shallow body of water formed by melting glaciers or floodwaters. When glaciers retreat, they will sometimes form small depressions called kettle holes. Then water flows into the kettle hole to create a kettle. A kettle with an inflow of water from a source other than rain would become a kettle lake. The Kettle Moraine in Wisconsin, the United States, contains many kettles.

Lacustrine Plain

A lacustrine plain is a plain formed by the filling with sediment and then drying out of a lake. The lake can be dried through drainage or evaporation. Kashmir Valley of India is an example of a lacustrine plain.

Lagoon

A lagoon is a body of shallow sea water or brackish water separated from the sea by some form of barrier. The Grand Lagon Sud in New Caledonia, France, is the largest lagoon in the world (1,214 sq mi / 3,145 km^2).

Lake

A lake is a body of relatively still fresh or salt water of considerable size, localized in a basin that is surrounded by land. Most lakes are fed and drained by rivers and streams.

Natural lakes are generally found in mountainous areas, rift zones, and areas with ongoing glaciations. Other lakes are found in endorheic basins or along the courses of mature rivers.

Largest lakes by area in the world:

- Caspian Sea – the largest lake in the world (143,000 sq mi / 371,000 km^2), endorheic and saline. It is located in Azerbaijan, Iran, Kazakhstan, Russia, and Turkmenistan.
- Lake Superior – the 2nd largest lake in the world (31,820 mi / 82,400 km²), glacial and freshwater. It is located in the United States and Canada.
- Lake Victoria – the 3rd largest lake in the world (26,600 sq mi / 68,800 km²), freshwater. It is located in Uganda, Kenya, and Tanzania.
- Lake Huron – the 4th largest lake in the world (23,012 sq mi / 59,600 km²), glacial and freshwater. It is located in the United States and Canada.
- Lake Michigan – the 5th largest lake in the world (22,317 sq mi / 57,800 km²), glacial and freshwater. It is located in the United States.
- Aral Sea – the 6th largest lake in the world (6,630 sq mi / 17,160 km^2), endorheic and saline. It is located in Russia.
- Lake Tanganyika – the 7th largest lake in the world (12,700 sq mi / 32,900 km^2), rift and freshwater. It is located in Burundi, Tanzania, Zambia, and Democratic Republic of the Congo.
- Lake Baikal – the 8th largest lake in the world (12,248 sq mi / 31,722 km^2), rift and freshwater. It is located in Russia.
- Great Bear Lake – the 9th largest lake in the world (12,021 sq mi / 31,153 km²), glacial and freshwater. It is located in Canada.
- Lake Malawi / Lake Nyasa – the 10th largest lake in the world (11,429 sq mi / 29,600 km²), rift and freshwater. It is located in Malawi, Mozambique, and Tanzania.

Largest lakes by volume in the world:

- Caspian Sea – the largest lake in the world (18,800 cu mi / 78,200 km^3). It is located in Azerbaijan, Iran, Kazakhstan, Russia, and Turkmenistan.
- Lake Baikal in Russia – the 2nd largest lake in the world (5,700 cu mi / 23,600 km^3).
- Lake Tanganyika – the 3rd largest lake in the world (4,500 cu mi / 18,900 km^3). It is located in Burundi, Tanzania, Zambia, and Democratic Republic of the Congo.
- Lake Superior – the 4th largest lake in the world (2,800 cu mi / 11,600 km^3). It is located in the United States and Canada.
- Lake Michigan – the 5th largest lake in the world (1,180 cu mi / 4,900 km^3). It is located in the United States.
- Lake Huron – the 6th largest lake in the world (849 cu mi / 3,539 km^3). It is located in the United States and Canada.
- Lake Malawi / Lake Nyasa – the 7th largest lake in the world (1,853 cu mi, 7,725 km^3). It is located in Malawi, Mozambique, and Tanzania.
- Vostok – the 8th largest lake in the world (1,300 cu mi / 5,400 km^3), subglacial and rift. It is located in Antarctica.
- Lake Victoria – the 9th largest lake in the world (650 cu mi / 2,700 km^3). It is located in Uganda, Kenya, and Tanzania.
- Great Bear Lake – the 10th largest lake in the world (536 cu mi / 2,236 km^3). It is located in Canada.

Deepest lakes in the world:

- Lake Baikal – the deepest lake in the world (5,369 ft / 1,637 m). It is located in Russia.
- Lake Tanganyika – the 2nd deepest lake in the world (4,823 ft / 1,470m). It is located in Burundi, Tanzania, Zambia, and Democratic Republic of the Congo.
- Caspian Sea – the 3rd deepest lake in the world (3,363 ft / 1,025m). It is located in Azerbaijan, Iran, Kazakhstan, Russia, and Turkmenistan.
- Vostok – the 4th deepest lake in the world (2,950 ft / 900 m). It is located in Antarctica.
- O'Higgins / San Martín Lake – the 5th deepest lake in the world (2,742 ft / 836 m), glacial and freshwater. It is located in Chile and Argentina.
- Lake Malawi / Lake Nyasa – the 6th deepest lake in the world (2,316 ft / 706 m). It is located in Malawi, Mozambique, and Tanzania.
- Issyk Kul – the 7th deepest lake in the world (2,192 ft / 668), endorheic and monomictic. It is located in Kyrgyzstan.
- Great Slave Lake – the 8th deepest lake in the world (2,015 ft / 614 m), glacial and freshwater. It is located in Canada.
- Crater Lake – the 9th deepest lake in the world (1,949 ft / 594 m), endorheic and crater. It is located in the United States.
- Lake Matano – the 10th deepest lake in the world (1,936 ft / 590 m), tectonic and freshwater. It is located in Indonesia.

Other facts:

- The longest lake is Lake Tanganyika (410 mi / 660 km).
- The oldest lake is Lake Baikal (25 million years old), followed by Lake Tanganyika (3 million years old).
- The highest lake is the crater lake of Ojos del Salado in Argentina and Chile (20,965 ft / 6,390 m), followed by the Lhagba Pool in China at (20,892 ft / 6,368 m).
- The highest large freshwater lake is Lake Manasarovar in China (14,948 ft / 4,556 m).
- The highest commercially navigable lake is Lake Titicaca in Peru and Bolivia (12,507 ft / 3,812 m).
- The lowest (elevation) lake is the Dead Sea in Israel, Jordan, and West Back (-1,339 ft / -408 m).
- Lake Huron has the longest lake coastline, excluding the coastline of its many inner islands (1,852 mi / 2,980 km).
- The largest island in a freshwater lake is Manitoulin Island in Lake Huron, with a surface area of (1,068 sq mi / 2,766 km²).
- Lake Manitou, located on Manitoulin Island, is the largest lake on an island in a freshwater lake.
- The largest lake located on an island is Nettilling Lake on Baffin Island, Canada (2,139 sq mi / 5,542 km²).
- The largest lake in the world that drains naturally in two directions is Wollaston Lake in Canada.
- Lake Toba on the island of Sumatra, Indonesia, is located in the largest resurgent caldera on Earth.
- The largest lake located completely within the boundaries of a single city is Lake Wanapitei in the city of Sudbury, Canada.
- Lake Enriquillo in Dominican Republic is the only saltwater lake in the world inhabited by crocodiles.
- Lake Bernard in Canada is the largest freshwater lake in the world with no islands.
- The largest lake in one country is Lake Michigan in the United States.
- Sometimes, Lake Michigan and Lake Huron are counted as a single lake since it is hydrologically a single body of water.
- The largest lake on an island in a lake on an island is Crater Lake on Vulcano Island in Lake Taal on the island of Luzon, Philippines.

Landform

Landform is a specific geomorphic feature on the surface of Earth.

Landforms can be organized by the processes that create them:

- Aeolian landforms – formed by the wind, aeolian landforms are barchan dune, blowout depression, desert pavement, desert varnish, dune, dreikanter, erg, loess, playa, sandhill, ventifact, and yardang.

- Coastal and oceanic landforms – occurs in coastal or oceanic environments, common landforms include abyssal fan, abyssal plain, archipelago, atoll, arch, ayre, barrier island, bay, beach, beach cusp, beach ridge, bight, bill, blowhole, channel, cape, cliff, coast, continental shelf, coral reef, cove, cuspate foreland, dune, estuary, firth, fjord, gulf, headland, inlet, island, island arc, islet, isthmus, lagoon, machair, marine terrace, mid-ocean ridge, ocean, oceanic basin, oceanic plateau, oceanic trench, peninsula, point, promontory, ria, delta, salt marsh, sea, sea cave, shoal, sound, spit, stack, strait, stump, submarine canyon, surge channel, tombolo, volcanic arc, and wave cut platform.
- Erosion landforms – formed by erosion and weathering, usually occur in coastal or fluvial environments, erosion landforms include arch, badland, bench, butte, canyon, cave, cliff, cuesta, dissected plateau, eolianite, erg, gulch, gully, hogback, hoodoo, karst, lavaka, limestone pavement, malpais, mesa, pediment, peneplain, potrero, ravine, ridge, roche moutonnée, sinkhole, tea table, tepui, and valley.
- Fluvial landforms – formed by erosion related to rivers and streams, fluvial landforms include ait, alluvial fan, anabranch, arroyo, bayou, bench, braided stream, cave, cliff, drainage basin, endorheic basin, exhumed river channel, natural levee, meander, oasis, oxbow lake, dry lake, pond, proglacial lake, promontory rapid, river, rock-cut basin, shoal, stream, swamp, towhead, valley, vale, and watershed.
- Mountain and glacier landforms – arête, cirque, crevasse, dirt cone, drumlin and drumlin field, esker, fjord, fluvial terrace, glacial horn, glacier, glacier cave, glacier foreland, hanging valley, hill, kame, kame delta, kettle, monadnock, moraine and ribbed moraines, moulin, mountain, mountain range, nunatak, outwash fan and outwash plain, pingo, rift valley, roche moutonnée, sandur, side valley, summit, trim line, tunnel valley, valley, and U-shaped valley.
- Slope landforms – alas, bluff, butte, cliff, cuesta, dale, defile, dell, escarpment, glen, gully, hill, knoll, mesa, mountain pass, plain, plateau, ravine, ridge, rock shelter, scree, strath, terrace and terracettes, vale, valley, and valley shoulder.
- Volcanic landforms – caldera, crater lake, geyser, lava dome, lava flow and lava plain, lava lake, lava spine, lava tube, maar, malpais, mamelon, mid-ocean ridge, oceanic trench, pit crater, pseudocrater, subglacial mound, tuya, vent, volcanic cone, volcanic craters, volcanic dam, volcanic field, volcanic group, volcanic island, volcanic plateau, and volcanic plug.

Landslide

A landslide is a phenomenon which involves the ground moving, usually consisting of rock, sediment, and/or debris slipping down a slope. Landslides typically occur after the land has been weakened by types of erosion. Landslides can create massive damage, as well as trigger tsunamis if the landslide occurs underwater.

Types of landslides:

- Debris flow – slurry land becomes saturated, making ground week and causing a flow of debris. It can also be called a mud flow.

- Earth flow – a downward flow of fine grainy materials. The speed of flow can be very slow or dangerously fast. Earth flows commonly occur after periods of heavy precipitation.
- Debris avalanche – a fast downward flow of rocks mixed with water or ice. Debris avalanches occur when a steep slope has been saturated, usually by water.
- Sturzstrom – a large landslide down a flat slope.
- Shallow landslide – a landslide where the sliding surface is located slightly underneath the surface. Water gets trapped under the soil, eventually making the ground saturated and susceptible to slippage.
- Deep-seated landslide – a landslide where the sliding surface is located 33 ft (10 m) or more below the surface. They are caused by weathered bedrock, but their depth makes their movement quite slow, usually a few feet per year.

La Niña

A La Niña occurs when winds transfer water, causing water to be colder on the east side of the Pacific and warmer on the west side of the Pacific Ocean. A La Niña tends to cause the opposite effects of El Niño's.

Latitude

Latitude is a term to locate an area's distance from the equator, measured in degrees north or south. Latitude goes from 0 degrees, the equator to 90 degrees, the North or South Pole. Latitude lines are all parallel with each other.

Important lines of latitude:

- 66° 33' 39" N – the Arctic Circle, lands farther north than this line get 24 hours of sunlight during summer and 24 hours of nighttime in the winter.
- 23° 26' 21" N – the Tropic of Cancer, marks the north end of the tropical zone.
- 0° – the equator, the only points on Earth not marked north or south. Separates the north and south hemispheres.
- 23° 26' 21" S – the Tropic of Capricorn, marks the south end of the tropical zone.
- 66° 33' 39" S – the Antarctic Circle, same as Arctic Circle but opposite.

Lava

Lava is the molten magma released from a volcanic vent.

Lava Channel

A lava channel is a stream of lava contained between clumps of cooled lava or levees.

Lava Dome

A lava dome is a roughly mound-shaped protrusion resulting from the slow outward flow of lava from a volcano. Lassen Peak in California is one of the largest lava domes in the world.

Lava Flow
A lava flow is a moving outpouring of lava, which is created during a non-explosive eruption. Lava flows solidify to form igneous rock.

Lavaka
Lavaka is a hole or gully formed by groundwater flow, with steep or vertical sides and flat floors. Lavakas have an inverted teardrop shape, with a wide headwall, and narrow, deeply incised outfall. Lavaka is common in Madagascar.

Lava Lake
A lava lake is a large volume of molten lava, contained in a volcanic vent, crater, or broad depression.

Active volcanoes with lava lakes in the world:

- Erta Ale in Ethiopia
- Mount Erebus in Antarctica
- Kilauea in Hawaii, the United States
- Nyiragongo in Democratic Republic of the Congo
- Marum on the island of Ambrym in Vanuatu
- Villarrica in Chile

Lava Plain
A lava plain is a large expanse of nearly flat-lying lava flows. It is also called a lava field or lava bed. The Hell's Half Acre lava field in Idaho, the United States, is an example of a lava plain.

Lava Spine
A lava spine is a standing cylindrical body of lava caused by lava being squeezed out from a volcanic vent. A 49 ft (15 m) high lava spine grew from the Mount Saint Helens eruption in Washington, the United States, in 1981.

Lava Tube
A lava tube is a natural pipe under the surface of a lava flow through which lava travels, expelled by a volcano during an eruption. Lava tubes can refer to lava tubes with lava still flowing through or ones that no longer contain lava.

Longest lava tubes in the world:

- Kazumura Cave – the longest lava tube in the world (41 mi /65,500 m), and also the deepest lava tube (3,614 ft / 1,102 m). It is located in Hawaii, the United States.
- Kipuka Kanohina – the 2nd longest lava tube in the world (length: 29 mi / 46,188 m, depth: 762 ft / 232 m). It is located in Hawaii, the United States.

- Reseau du Verneau – the 3rd longest lava tube in the world (length: 21 mi / 33,300 m, depth: 1,270 ft / 387 m). It is located in France.
- Reseau de Coufin-Chevaline – the 4th longest lava tube in the world (length: 19 mi / 29,839 m, depth: 1,348 ft / 411 m). It is located in France.
- Hualalai Ranch Cave – the 5th longest lava tube in the world (length: 17 mi / 27,785 m, depth: 1,449 ft / 442 m). It is located in Hawaii, the United States.
- Reseau de Bunant – the 6th longest lava tube in the world (length: 16 mi / 26,128 m, depth: 1,188 ft / 362 m). It is located in France.
- Emesine Cave – the 7th longest lava tube in the world (length: 13 mi / 20,744 m, depth: 1,433 ft / 437 m). It is located in Hawaii, the United States.
- Cueva del Viento-cueva del Sobrado – the 8th longest lava tube in the world (length: 11 mi / 18,000 m, depth: 1,837 ft / 560 m). It is located on Canary Islands, Spain.
- Aven du Sotch de la Tride – the 9th longest lava tube in the world (length: 11 mi / 17,400 m, depth: 1,122 ft / 342 m). It is located in France.
- Aven de la Leicasse – the 10th longest lava tube in the world (length: 10 mi / 16,530 m, depth: 1,168 ft / 356 m). It is located in France.
- Surtshellir-Stepanshellir et Hulduhellir – the 27th longest lava tube in the world (length: 3 mi / 5,000 m). Surtshellir-Stepanshellir et Hulduhellir was considered the longest lava tube until the end of the 19th century, but was broken into three pieces: Surtshellir-Stefanshellir-Ishellir. It is located in Iceland.

Limestone Pavement

A limestone pavement is a natural karst formed by acid rain, consisting of a flat, incised surface of exposed limestone that resembles an artificial pavement. Limestone pavements can be found in many previously-glaciated limestone environments around the world.

Loess

Loess is formed by the accumulation of wind-blown silt, and lesser and variable amounts of sand and clay. The Crowley's Ridge in Arkansas, the United States, is a natural loess accumulation point. There are volcanic loess in Ecuador, tropical loess in northeastern Argentina, Brazil and Uruguay, gypsum loess in northern Spain, trade-wind deposits in Venezuela and Brazil, and anticyclonic gray loess in Argentina.

Longitude

Longitude is a location's angular distance east or west of the meridian at Greenwich, the United Kingdom, on the Earth's surface. All longitude lines start at the North Pole down to the South Pole and are measured in degrees west or east. 0° is the prime meridian, which divides the west and east hemispheres of Earth. Longitude coordinates can go up to 180° to either direction.

Longshore Current

A longshore current is a water current that moves parallel to the shoreline.

Longshore Drift
The longshore drift is the movement and deposition of coastal sediments of longshore currents. The direction of longshore drift is dependent on prevailing wind direction, swash and backwash.

Longshore Transport
The longshore transport refers to the transport of sediment in water parallel to a shoreline.

Maar
A maar is a broad, low-relief volcanic crater that is caused by a phreatomagmatic eruption, an explosion caused by groundwater coming into contact with hot lava or magma. A maar is often filled with water to form a relatively shallow crater lake.

The Devil Mountain Lakes in the Seward Peninsula in Alaska, the United States, is the largest maar in the world (diameter: 5 mi / 8 km). There are double craters (North Devil Mountain maar and South Devil Mountain maar) in the lake. The Espenberg Maars, including the Killeak Lakes (North Killeak maar and South Killeak maar) and White Fish Lake (Whitefish Maar) are also located in the Seward Peninsula.

Machair
A machair is a type of fertile low-lying grassy plain on some of the northwestern coastlines of Ireland and Scotland. The machair is located on Berneray in the Outer Hebrides, Scotland.

Malpais
A malpais is a landform characterized by eroded rocks of volcanic origin in an arid environment.

Malpais examples:

- El Malpais National Monument in New Mexico, the United States
- Carrizozo Malpaís and Jornada del Muerto Volcano lava plain in New Mexico, the United States
- Malpaís de Güímar on Canary Islands, Spanish

Mamelon
A mamelon is a hill-like formation created by an eruption of relatively thick lava through a volcanic vent.

Mamelon examples:

- Mamelon Central in the Piton de la Fournaise volcano on Réunion, France
- Hanging Rock in Australia

Marsh
A marsh is a type of wetland susceptible to frequent floods. Marshes have shallow water and contain mostly grass, reeds, herbaceous plants, and moss.

Mass Wasting
Mass wasting is a general term that describes the downward slope movement of sediment, soil, and rock material under the force of gravity. The types of mass wasting include creep, slides, and flows, topple, and fall. It can take place over timescales from seconds to years, on land or underwater. Mass wasting is also called slope movement or mass movement.

Examples of mass wasting:

- Palo Duro Canyon in Texas, the United States
- Grand Canyon National Park in Arizona, the United States
- Talus cones at north shore of Isfjord on the island of Svalbard, Norway

Meander
A meander is a curve in a watercourse due to erosion through a flat area. The meander will gradually get curvier until the curve is broken away into an oxbow lake. Meanders can also be incised, which means flowing downwards into the ground.

Mesa
A mesa is an elevated area of land with a flat top and sides that are usually steep cliffs. As a mesa erodes away further, it can become a butte. The Grand Mesa in Colorado, the United States, is the largest mesa by area in the world (500 sq mi / 1300 km²).

Mid-Ocean Ridge
A mid-ocean ridge (MOR) is an underwater mountain system that consists of various mountain ranges (chains), formed by plate tectonics. The mid-ocean ridges of the world are connected and form a single global mid-oceanic ridge system that is part of every ocean, making the mid-oceanic ridge system the longest mountain range in the world (40,400 mi / 65,000 km).

Major mid-ocean ridges in the world:

- Aden Ridge – a divergent plate boundary that stretches from the Gulf of Aden through to Indian Ocean towards the Arabian Peninsula.
- Explorer Ridge – a divergent plate boundary that stretches off Vancouver Island west of Canada.
- Gorda Ridge – a divergent plate boundary that extends from the coast of northern California to Oregon, the United States.
- Juan de Fuca Ridge – a divergent plate boundary between Washington and

southwest Canada.
- Cocos Ridge – a divergent plate boundary which formed a hotspot at the Galapagos Islands.
- American-Antarctic Ridge – a plate boundary separating the South American Plate and the Antarctic Plate.
- Chile Rise – a plate boundary separating the Nazca Plate (Peru) and the Antarctic Plate.
- East Pacific Rise – a divergent plate boundary separating six different plates in the South American region.
- East Scotia Ridge – a divergent plate boundary in the South Atlantic Ocean.
- Gakkel Ridge (Mid-Arctic Ridge) – a divergent plate boundary in the Arctic Ocean separating the North American Plate and Eurasian Plate.
- Pacific-Antarctic Ridge – a divergent plate boundary in the South Pacific Ocean separating the Pacific and Antarctic plates.
- Southeast Indian Ridge – a divergent plate boundary in the southern Indian Ocean separating the Indo-Australian Plate from the Antarctic Plate.
- Central Indian Ridge – a divergent plate boundary in the western Indian Ocean separating the African and Indo-Australian Plate.
- Southwest Indian Ridge – a divergent plate boundary south of the Central Indian Ridge. It also separates the same two plates.
- Mid-Atlantic Ridge – a divergent plate boundary that stretches all the way across the Atlantic Ocean, stretching from the Gakkel Range in the Arctic Ocean down to the Antarctic plate.

Mineral

A mineral is a naturally occurring solid chemical substance that is formed through geological processes and that has a characteristic chemical composition, a highly ordered atomic structure, and specific physical properties.

Minerals can be classified into different chemical classes: silicate class, carbonate class, sulfate class, halide class, oxide class, sulfide class, phosphate class, element class, and organic class. More than 95% rocks are silicates.

Physical properties of a mineral:

- Crystal structure – the orderly geometric spatial arrangement of atoms in the internal structure of a mineral.
- Crystal habit – the form of massive, granular or compact with only microscopically visible crystals.
- Hardness – the physical hardness of a mineral is usually measured according to the Mohs scale (1 – 10, and 10 is the hardest, such as diamond).
- Luster – the way a mineral's surface interacts with light and can range from dull to glassy (vitreous).
- Diaphaneity – how well light passes through a mineral (transparent, translucent,

and opaque).
- Color – the appearance of the mineral in reflected light or transmitted light.
- Streak – the color of the powder a mineral leaves after rubbing it on an unglazed porcelain streak plate.
- Cleavage – the way a mineral may split apart along various planes.
- Fracture – how a mineral breaks when broken contrary to its natural cleavage planes (chonchoidal, hackley, fibrous, and irregular).
- Specific gravity – the mineral mass to the mass of an equal volume of water, namely the density of the material (Most minerals have a specific gravity of 2.5 – 3.5).
- Fluorescence – the response to ultraviolet light.
- Magnetism – the response to an applied magnetic field.
- Radioactivity – how unstable atoms lose energy by emitting ionizing particles.
- Tenacity – the response to mechanical induced changes of shape or form.
- Piezoelectricity – the charge in response to applied mechanical strain.

Mineraloid

A mineraloid is a mineral-like substance that does not demonstrate crystallinity. Mineraloids possess chemical compositions that vary beyond the generally accepted ranges for specific minerals.

Common mineraloids:

- Amber – non-crystalline structure.
- Jet – non-crystalline nature, very compact coal.
- Native mercury – liquid, IMA/CNMNC valid mineral name.
- Lechatelierite – nearly pure silica glass.
- Limonite – a mixture of oxides.
- Lapis Lazuli – a mix of minerals.
- Obsidian – volcanic glass, non-crystalline structure, a glass and quartz mixture.
- Opal – non-crystalline silicon dioxide, a mix of minerals, IMA/CNMNC valid mineral name.
- Pearl – organically produced carbonate.
- Petroleum – liquid.
- Pyrobitumen – non-homogeneous, non-crystalline structure, doesn't melt by heating.
- Vulcanite – vulcanized natural or synthetic rubber, thus not a mineral due to lack of crystalline structure.
- Tektites – meteoritic silica glass.

Monadnock

A monadnock is an isolated hill that suddenly rises among an area of flat land. A monadnock is formed when the rock in the certain area is strengthened, sometimes by volcanic activity. When forces of erosion erode the surrounding areas, the monadnock survives and becomes taller than the surrounding softer area. The Pilot Mountain in North Carolina, the United States, and the Sugarloaf Mountain in Brazil are examples of Monadnocks.

Moraine
A moraine is a hill of unconsolidated glacial debris (soil and rock), deposited directly by a glacier. Moraines are a part of the formation of many glacial landforms. The Waterloo Moraine is located in Canada.

Moulin
A moulin is a crevasse that forms at the surface of a glacier down towards the rock underneath. Moulins are responsible for glacial landforms like glacier caves as it allows the water to go down to the bottom of the glacier, allowing the water to carve the previously unreachable ice.

Mountain
A mountain is a landform that stretches high above the surrounding areas forming one or several peaks. Its slope is typically steeper than a hill's. There are many differing parameters on what makes a mountain, but it usually involves the peak being several thousand feet above sea level.

Types of mountains:

- Fold mountain – created by a collision between two tectonic plates, causing the plates to fold up. The Himalayan Mountains in Asia is an example of a fold mountain.
- Fault-block mountain – created by rock materials that move along faults. The Sierra Nevada mountain chain in California, the United States, is an example of a fault-block mountain.
- Volcanic mountain – created by volcanic eruptions by the lava that hardens after it reaches the surface. Mount Fuji in Japan is an example of a volcanic mountain.
- Dome mountain – created by a push of magma underneath the ground to lift the sediments above it into a peak. The resulting mountain usually is in a dome shape. The Navajo Mountain in Utah, the United States is an example of a dome mountain.
- Plateau mountain – created by erosion. The Adirondack Mountains in New York, the United States, is an example of a plateau mountain.

Tallest mountains in the world:

- Mount Everest – the tallest mountain in the world (29,029 ft / 8,848 m). Mount Everest grows slightly taller every year. It is located in China and Nepal.
- K2 – the 2nd tallest mountain in the world (28,251 ft / 8,611 m). It is located in

China and Pakistan.
- Kangchenjunga – the 3rd tallest mountain in the world (28,169 ft / 8,450 m). It is located in India and Nepal.
- Lhotse – the 4th tallest mountain in the world (27,503 ft / 8,383 m). It is located in China and Nepal.
- Makalu – the 5th tallest mountain in the world (27,825 ft / 8,481 m). It is located in China and Nepal.
- Cho Oyu – It is the 6th tallest mountain in the world (26,906 ft / 8,201 m). It is located in China and Nepal.
- Dhaulagiri I – the 7th tallest mountain in the world (26,795 ft / 8,167 m). It is located in Nepal.
- Manaslu – the 8th tallest mountain in the world (26,759 ft / 8,156 m). It is located in Nepal.
- Nanga Parbat – the 9th tallest mountain in the world (26,660 ft / 8,126 m). It is located in Pakistan.
- Annapurna I – the 10th tallest mountain in the world (26,545 ft / 8,091 m). It is located in Nepal.
- Aconcagua – the tallest mountain in South America (22,834 ft / 6,960 m). It is located in Argentina.
- Mount McKinley – the tallest mountain in North America (20,335 ft / 6,198 m). It is located in Alaska, the United States.
- Mount Elbrus – the tallest mountain in Europe (18,510 ft / 5,642 m). It is located in Russia.
- Vinson Massif – the tallest mountain in Antarctica (16,066 ft / 4,896 m). It is located in Antarctica.
- Mount Kosciuszko – the tallest mountain in Oceania (7,310 ft / 2,228 m). It is located in Australia.

Major mountain chains in the world:

- Mid-Atlantic Range – underwater mountain range running through the Atlantic Ocean. It is the longest mountain range in the world (40,389 mi / 65,000 km).
- Andes – runs through the western side of South America. It is the 2nd longest mountain range and longest above water (4,350 mi / 7000 km).
- Rocky Mountains – runs through the continent of North America from Canada down to Mexico. It is the 3rd longest mountain range in the world (2,983 mi / 4,800 km).
- Great Dividing Range – runs through eastern Australia. It is the 4th longest mountain range in the world (2,299 mi / 3,700 km).
- Transantarctic Mountains – runs through Antarctica. It is the 5th longest mountain range in the world (2,175 mi / 3,500 km).
- Himalaya Mountains – runs through Central Asia. It is the 6th longest mountain range in the world (1,491 mi / 2,400 km). It is also the tallest mountain chain in the world.
- Alps – runs through Western Europe. Most famous mountain chain in Europe.

Névé

Névé is a young, granular type of snow which has been partially melted, refrozen and compacted, yet precedes the form of ice. It is associated with glacier formation through the process of nivation. Névé has a minimum density of 31 lb / ft³ (500 kg / m³). The Névé Glacier in Washington, the United States, is located in North Cascades National Park.

Nivation

Nivation is a collective name for the different processes that occur under a snow patch. During these processes, the fallen snow gets compacted into firn or névé. The term glacier is applied only when ice has accumulated enough for the mass to achieve motion.

Oasis

An oasis is an isolated area of vegetation in a desert. The water in oases typically comes from a spring. Oases are usually created when an artesian well undergoes pressure, forcing water upwards to the surface. Plants usually start growing from seeds in bird droppings.

Notable oases in Africa:

- Nile River valley and delta – follows the Nile River as it flows through the desert that covers most of Egypt. It is considered to be the largest oasis in the world.
- Bahariya Oasis – located in central Egypt.
- Farafra Oasis – located slightly south of the Bahariya Oasis in Egypt.
- Gaberoun – located in the middle of the Libyan Sahara.
- Kufra Oasis – located in the middle of the Kufra basin in southeastern Libya.
- M'Zab Valley – located in the middle of the Sahara Desert in northern Algeria.
- Ouargla – located in the middle of the Sahara Desert in southern Algeria.
- Siwa Oasis – located in the Libyan Desert in western Egypt.
- Tafilalt – located in the Sahara Desert in southeast Morocco.
- Timimoun – located in central Algeria.
- Tozeur – located in Tunisia. The city of Tozeur lies next to the oasis.
- Tuat – located in the middle of the Sahara Desert in central Algeria.

Notable oases in the Americas:

- Fish Springs National Wildlife Refuge – located in the Great Basin in Utah, the United States.
- Huacachina – located in southwestern Peru.
- La Cienega – located in New Mexico, the United States, close to the city of Santa Fe.
- Las Vegas Valley – located in the Great Basin in Nevada, the United States. The city of Las Vegas is built around the oasis.
- Mulege – located in the Baja California Sur in Mexico.
- San Ignacio – located near Mulege in Mexico.

- San Pedro de Atacama – located in the Atacama Desert in Chile.
- Twentynine Palms – located in the Mojave Desert in southeastern California, the United States.
- Warm Springs Natural Area – located in the Mojave Desert in Nevada, the United States.

Notable oases in Asia:

- Al-Hasa – located in the Arabian Desert in eastern Saudi Arabia. It is the largest oasis in Asia.
- Al-Qatif – located in the Arabian Desert in eastern Saudi Arabia.
- Azraq – located in Jordan.
- Ein Gedi – located in Israel located slightly east of the Dead Sea.
- Liwa Oasis – located in the United Arab Emirates.
- Loulan – located on the Silk Road in northwestern China.
- Miran – located in the Taklamakan Desert in western China.
- Niya – located in the Tarim Basin in western China
- Tabas – located in eastern Iran.
- Turpan – located on the Silk Road in northwestern China.
- Yarkand – located in the Taklamakan Desert in western China. It is fed by the Yarkand River.

Notable oasis in Oceania:

- Palm Valley – located in the dry Northern Territories of Australia.

Notable oasis in Europe:

- Herðubreiðarlindir – located in the middle of a volcanic area in Iceland.

Ocean
An ocean is a major body of saline water. There are five oceans overall: the Pacific Ocean, the Atlantic Ocean, the Indian Ocean, the Arctic Ocean, and the Southern Ocean, though they are all interconnected. Together, they cover 71% of the Earth's surface.

Ocean Basin
The ocean basin is part of the Earth's outer surface that is comprised of the ocean floor, mid-oceanic ridges, continental rise, and continental slope. The ocean basins are filled with saline water that makes up the oceans.

Major ocean basins in the world:

- South Atlantic Ocean – Agulhas Basin, Angola Basin, Argentine Basin, and Chile

- Basin
- North Atlantic Ocean – Canary Basin, Cascadia Basin, Brazil Basin, and Eurasian Basin (Nansen Basin and the Fram Basin), Guiana Basin, Herodotus Basin, Labrador Basin, Rhodes Basin, Sierra Leone Basin, Mexico Basin, and Sirte Basin
- Southern Ocean – Cape Basin
- Arctic Ocean – Amerasian Basin (Canada Basin and Makarov Basin), Gambia Basin, Iceland Basin, and Central Polar Basin
- Indian Ocean – Madagascar Basin, Mid-Indian Basin, Natal Basin, Arabian Basin, Perth Basin, and Somali Basin
- Southern Ocean – South Indian Basin
- Pacific Ocean – Aleutian Basin, Bauer Basin, Central Pacific Basin, Melanesian Basin, Northwest Pacific Basin, Penrhyn Basin, Peru Basin, Roggeveen Basin, South China Basin, South East Pacific Basin, South Fiji Basin, South West Pacific Basin, Tasman Basin, Tsushima Basin, and Yamato Basin

Oceanic crust

Oceanic crust is the Earth's outermost shell that surfaces in the ocean basins. It is thinner and denser than continental crust. The oceanic crust is generally less than 6 mi (10 km) thick.

Oceanic Plateau

An oceanic plateau is a large, relatively flat submarine region that rises well above the level of the ambient seabed. The Ontong Java-Manihiki-Hikurangi is the largest oceanic plateau (800,000 sq mi / 2,000,000 km²).

Major oceanic plateaus in the world:

- North Atlantic Ocean – Caribbean-Colombian Plateau and Vøring Plateau
- Indian Ocean – Agulhas Plateau, Exmouth Plateau, Kerguelen Plateau, Mascarene Plateau, and Naturaliste Plateau
- Pacific Ocean – Campbell Plateau, Challenger Plateau, Hikurangi Plateau, Manihiki Plateau, Marquesas Plateau, Ontong Java Plateau, Shatsky Rise, and Wrangellia Terrane
- Arctic Ocean – Yermak Plateau

Oceanic Trench

An oceanic trench is a deep depression found at the edge of the ocean floor.

Deepest oceanic trenches in the world:

- Mariana Trench in Pacific Ocean (36,198 ft / 11,033 m)
- Tonga Trench in Pacific Ocean (35,702 ft / 10,882 m)
- Kuril–Kamchatka Trench in Pacific Ocean (34,587 ft / 10,542 m)

- Philippine Trench in Pacific Ocean (34,580 ft / 10,540 m)
- Kermadec Trench in Pacific Ocean (32,963 ft / 10,047 m)
- Izu-Bonin Trench in Pacific Ocean (32,090 ft / 9,780 m)
- Japan Trench in Pacific Ocean (30,000 ft / 9,000 m)
- Puerto Rico Trench in Atlantic Ocean (28,232 ft / 8,605 m)
- Peru-Chile Trench in Pacific Ocean (26,460 ft / 8,065 m)

The Challenger Deep in the Mariana Trench is the deepest point on Earth (36,198 ft / 11,033 m).

Oxbow Lake

An oxbow lake is a body of water formed when a meander of a river is cut off. It is formed because of a river's tendency to curve more and more in flat areas. There are many oxbow lakes in the vicinity of the Mississippi River.

Pediment

A pediment is a gently inclined erosional surface carved into bedrock. Grove Karl Gilbert first observed pediments in the Henry Mountains in Utah, the United States, in 1877.

Peneplain

A peneplain is a relatively flat land surface produced by a long period of fluvial erosion. The remnants of a peneplain were uplifted to form the Allegheny Plateau, the United States.

Peninsula

A peninsula is a piece of land surrounded by water on three of its sides and connected with a larger landmass on its fourth side. A peninsula can also be called a headland, cape, promontory, bill, point, or spit.

Largest peninsulas in the world:

- Arabian Peninsula (1,250,000 sq mi / 3,237,500 km^2)
- Southern India Peninsula (800,000 sq mi / 2,072,000 km^2)
- Alaska Peninsula (580,000 sq mi / 1,502,200 km^2)
- Labrador Peninsula (502,000 sq mi / 1,300,180 km^2)
- Scandinavia Peninsula (309,000 sq mi / 800,310 km^2)
- Iberian Peninsula (225,000 sq mi / 582,750 km^2)

Pingo

A pingo is a mound of earth-covered ice. Pingos are typically found in arctic or subarctic areas, as they can only occur in areas of permafrost. If the area heats up and the ice melts, the pingo will collapse. Pingos can have a round top, a top crusted with ice not fully covered, or have craters if collapsed. There are many pingos in northern Canada and Greenland.

Pit Crater
A crater formed by sinking in of the surface, not primarily a vent for lava. Hawaii, the United States, is known for its pit craters, such as Devil's Throat.

Plain
A plain is an area of relative flatness, usually rich in sediments. Plains can occur at any elevation, from plains at the ocean floor to the top of plateaus.

Types of plains:

- Coastal plain – an area of flat land near the sea. It is usually called a coastal plain when land inland consists of hills or other landforms with varying elevation.
- Alluvial plain – an area of flat land caused by rivers. It is usually called the floodplain, the sides of the river where flooding often occurs. However, there are also scroll plains, which is the plain next to the river when the river meanders slowly downwards.
- Lacustrine plain – a plain that is formed from the remnants of a lake bed.
- Lava plain – a plain formed by cooled lava after volcanic activity.
- Glacial plain – a plain formed by glacial activity. There are two types of glacial plains, a till plain where an outcrop of a glacier melts and deposits sediments, and a sandur where the sediment is deposited by meltwater.
- Abyssal plain – a plain that is underwater.

Playa
A playa is a sandy, salty, or mud-caked flat floor of a desert basin having interior drainage, usually occupied by a shallow lake during or after prolonged, heavy rains. It is also called dry lake, alkali flat, sabkha, playa or mud flat. The Salar de Uyuni in Bolivia is the largest salt flat by size in the world (4,085 sq mi / 10,582 km^2).

Plateau
A plateau is an area of highland, usually consisting of relatively flat terrain.

Plateaus can be classified based on the methods of formation:

- Plateaus formed by lava – lava comes out of the surface of the earth through zones of weakness. This lava spreads in the surroundings areas and forms plateau. The Southern Plateau (Malwa Plateau and Deccan Plateau) in India and the Columbia Plateau in the United States are lava plateaus.
- Plateaus formed by Running Water – high Mountains are eroded down by rivers. Plateau is formed as a landform by the advanced erosion. The Brazil Plateau in Brazil is such a plateau.
- Plateaus formed by Glaciers – glaciers form by deposition and erosion. The plateaus

of Russia and Finland are formed by deposition. The plateaus of Greenland and Antarctica formed by erosion.
- Plateaus formed by Wind – when winds blow from a desert in a certain direction, fine dust particles along with the winds reach far-off places. The Loess Plateau in China and Potwar plateau in Pakistan were formed by the wind erosion.

Plateaus can also be classified based on their surrounding environment:

- Intermontane Plateaus – these plateaus are the highest in the world, bordered by mountains, e.g. the plateaus in Bolivia, China, Peru, and Mexico.
- Piedmont Plateaus – these plateaus are bordered on one side by mountains and on the other by a plain or sea, e.g. the plateaus in Colorado (the United States) and Patagonia (South America).
- Continental Plateaus – these plateaus are bordered on all sides by the plains or seas, formed away from mountains, e.g. the Deccan Plateau in India, the Arab plateau, and the plateaus of Spain and Australia.

Largest plateaus in the world:

- Tibetan Plateau – the largest plateau in the world, and also the highest plateau in the world. It is located in China and Kashmir.
- Antarctic Plateau – the 2nd largest plateau in the world. It covers the South Pole.
- Andean Plateau – the 3rd largest plateau in the world. It is located in Bolivia, Colombia, Ecuador, Peru, Chile and Argentina.

Point
A point is another term for peninsula. Eye Peninsula in the Outer Hebrides, Scotland, is called a point.

Pond
A pond is a small standing body of water. A pond can occur naturally through an accumulation of precipitation or can also be manmade. Many ponds do not have an outflow.

Potrero
A potrero is a long mesa that at one end slopes upward to higher terrain. Many mesas of the Pajarito Plateau in New Mexico, the United States, are potreros.

Proglacial Lake
A proglacial lake is a lake formed by the remnants of a melting glacier. The water is held in by the moraines or ice dam. Proglacial lakes are typically created in a period where Earth is getting warmer, such as at the end of an Ice Age. Lake Harrison, Lake Lapworth, and Lake Pickering in the United Kingdom are some examples of proglacial lakes.

Promontory
A promontory is a prominent mass of land which overlooks lower lying land or a body of water. They are usually formed because some parts of the rock are less easily eroded than other sections. The Wilsons Promontory is located in southern Australia.

Pseudocrater
A pseudocrater is a volcanic landform which resembles a volcanic crater, but differs in that it is not an actual vent from which lava has erupted. Pseudocraters are formed by steam explosions as flowing hot lava crosses over a wet surface, such as a swamp, a lake, or a pond. The explosive gases break through the lava surface in a manner similar to a phreatic eruption, and the tephra builds up crater-like forms which can appear very similar to real volcanic craters. There are a lot of pseudocraters in Iceland: Lake Mývatn, Rauðhólar, Landbrotshólar, and Eyjafjallajökull.

Pyramidal Peak
A pyramidal peak is a mountain peak that is shaped by multiple glaciers, usually three or more. Glaciers usually erode all sides of the mountain slope, creating cirques, resulting in a strange pyramidal shaped peak. The Grand Teton in Wyoming, the United States, is an example of a pyramidal peak.

Rainforest
Rainforests are forests that get at least 68 in – 78 in (1.7 m – 2.0 m) of rain per year. Rainforests contain a lot of biodiversity and is vital to the oxygen supply for Earth. There are two types of rainforests, tropical or temperate. A tropical rainforest is a rainforest that is in the tropical zone, the area between the lines of tropic of Capricorn and Cancer. A famous tropical rainforest is the Amazon Rainforest in South America. A temperate rainforest is a rainforest in a temperate zone. There is a temperate rainforest in the Pacific Northwest region of the United States.

Rapid
A rapid is a section of a river where the slope is steeper, causing the water to travel faster than other areas. Rapids tend to be shallower than other places of a river. Whitewater is usually present in the faster rapids.

Ravine
A ravine is generally a fluvial slope landform of relatively steep sides. A ravine is larger than a gully and smaller than a valley. It is also narrower than a canyon, and is often the product of stream cutting erosion. The Homole Ravine is in located in Poland, the United States.

Reef
A reef is a rock or other object that lies just under the oceans' surface. Reefs can be living as well, the most well-known being a coral reef. There are numerous rock reefs in the Great

Salt Lake in Utah, the United States.

Ria
A ria is a drowned river valley created when the sea level rises. Both rias and fjords are formed in drowned valleys, but rias are formed by rivers while fjords are formed by glaciers. The Georges River in Sydney, Australia, is a ria.

Ridge
A ridge is a long, narrow upper section or crest. A ridge may refer to a chain of mountains or hills that are of a continuous elevated crest for some distance. A ridge is also a long, narrow elevation on the ocean floor.

Rift Valley
A rift valley is a linear shaped lowland between a set of mountains or other elevated land as a result of tectonic activity. The elevated land can also be underwater, as ocean tectonic plates can also form rift valleys. Rift valleys can start very thin but will eventually get wider as erosion occurs due to the sloped nature of the area. Rift valleys can be filled to create lakes. Some notable rift valley lakes are Lake Baikal in Russia and Lake Tanganyika in southern Africa. The East African Rift Valley and the mid-Atlantic range are examples of rift valleys.

River
A river is a natural watercourse, usually freshwater, flowing towards an ocean, a lake, a sea, another river, or drying up completely. Small rivers may also be called as stream, creek, brook, rivulet, tributary and rill. River length is usually measured by the total length from the source all the way to the mouth, though some sources measure the river differently or exclude a section of it as a different river, so some discrepancy exists between different sources. If there is more than one branch of the river merging, the branch with the higher water flow is considered to be part of the main river (tracing up the river) while the other branch is considered to be a tributary of the main river.

Longest rivers in the world:

- Nile River – the longest river in the world (4,132 mi / 6,650 km). It has sources in Ethiopia as well as Lake Victoria, which form the two main branches of the Nile, the Blue Nile and the White Nile. The Nile River also travels through Sudan, South Sudan, Egypt, Rwanda, Tanzania, Uganda, Burundi, Democratic Republic of the Congo, Eritrea, and Kenya, eventually entering the Mediterranean Sea in Egypt.
- Amazon River – the 2nd longest river in the world (4,000 mi / 6,437 km), and also the largest river by water flow. It has its source in Peru, and then flows through Colombia and Brazil into the Atlantic Ocean.
- Yangtze River – the 3rd longest river in the world (3,915 mi / 6,300 km). It has its source in the Tanggula Mountains in China and empties out into the East China Sea.

- Jefferson-Missouri-Mississippi – the 4th longest river in the world (3,900 mi / 6,300 km). It is located in the United States.
- Yenisey River – the 5th longest river in the world (3,534 mi / 5,526 km). It is located in Russia.
- Yellow River – the 6th longest river in the world (3,395 mi / 5,464 km). It has its source in the Bayan Har Mountains in China and flows eastward into the East China Sea.
- Ob-Irtysh River – the 7th longest river in the world (3,354 mi / 5,398 km). It is located in Russia.
- Congo River (also called Zaire River) – the 8th longest river in the world (2,922 mi / 4,700 km). It is located in Angola, Burundi, Cameroon, Central African Republic, Democratic Republic of the Congo, Gabon, Republic of the Congo, Rwanda, Tanzania, and Zambia.
- Amur Darya (also called Heilong) – the 9th longest river in the world (2,744 mi / 4,416 km). It is located in Mongolia, Russia, and China.
- Lena River – the 10th longest river in the world (2,734 mi / 4,400 km). It is located in Russia.

Other notable rivers:

- Fly River – the largest river in Oceania by water discharge, and also the largest river in the world without a dam. It flows through Papua New Guinea, briefly making the border with Indonesia before flowing eastward out into Gulf of Papua.
- Niger River – the 3rd longest river in Africa. It starts in Guinea and flows eastward through Mali, Niger, and Benin before flowing southward into the Gulf of Guinea in Nigeria.
- Volga River – the longest river in Europe. The river starts in the Valdai Hills and then flows southward to the Caspian Sea.
- Danube River – the 2nd longest river in Europe. The river starts in Black Forest, Germany and then continues to flow through Austria, Slovakia, Hungary, Croatia, Serbia, Bulgaria, Moldova, Ukraine, and Romania, where it flows into the Black Sea. Because it flows through so many different countries, as well as 4 capital cities, the Danube is considered to be one of the most important rivers in the world.
- Rhine River – a major River of Europe. The river starts in the Swiss Alps in Switzerland and then flows through Liechtenstein, Austria, France, Germany, and the Netherlands, where it joins the North Sea.
- Po River – a major river of Italy. The river starts in the Cottian Alps in Italy and flows into the Adriatic Sea at the city of Venice.
- Rhone River – a major river of Europe. The river starts at the Rhone Glacier in Switzerland, flows south into France, and empties into the Mediterranean Sea.
- Indus River – a major river of Asia. The river starts in the Tibetan Plateau in China, flows southwest through India and Pakistan, and empties into the Arabian Sea.
- Ganges River – a major river of Asia. The river starts in the Gangotri Glacier in India, flows into Bangladesh, and merges with the Brahmaputra River to form the biggest

- delta in the world.
- Ayeyarwady River – a major river in Asia. The river starts from the Mali River and stays within Myanmar until it empties out into the Andaman Sea.
- Mekong River – a major river in Asia and sometimes considered to be the 10th longest river in the world. The river starts off in China and then flows southeast through Myanmar, Laos, Thailand, and Cambodia before ending in Vietnam into the South China Sea.
- Tigris River – makes up the north and eastern border of the region called Mesopotamia, which is famous for its ancient civilization. The river starts in Turkey and goes through Syria and Iraq before joining the Euphrates River and emptying into the Arabian Sea.
- Euphrates River – makes up the south and western border of the region called Mesopotamia. The river, like the Tigris River, starts in Turkey and goes through Syria and Iraq and joins the Tigris River in southeastern Iraq before flowing into the Arabian Sea.
- Parana River – a major river in South America and sometimes considered to be the 8th longest river in the world. The river originates from the Paranaiba River in Brazil, flows through Paraguay and Argentina, and empties into the Rio De Plata.

Roche Moutonnée

A roche moutonnée is a rock formation created by the passing of a glacier. When a glacier erodes down to bedrock, it can form tear-drop shaped hills that taper in the up-ice direction. A roche moutonnée is also called a sheepback. There are roche moutonnées in Snowdonia National Park, the United Kingdom.

Rock

Rock is a naturally occurring solid aggregate of minerals and/or mineraloids. Rock is also called stone. There are three main rock types: sedimentary, metamorphic, and igneous. The transformation of one rock type to another is described by the geological model called the rock cycle.

Igneous rocks are formed when molten magma cools, and are divided into two main categories: plutonic rock and volcanic. Plutonic or intrusive rocks form when magma cools and crystallizes slowly within the Earth's crust. Granite is an example of a plutonic rock. Volcanic or extrusive rocks form when magma reaches the surface either as lava or fragmental ejecta. Pumice and basalt are examples of volcanic rocks.

Sedimentary rocks are formed by deposition of clastic sediments, organic matter, or chemical precipitates, followed by compaction of the particulate matter and cementation during diagenesis. Sedimentary rocks form at or near the Earth's surface. Mudstone, shale, siltstone, limestone and dolostone are examples of sedimentary rock.

Metamorphic rocks are formed by subjecting any rock type, including previously formed metamorphic rock, to different temperature and pressure conditions than those in which the original rock was formed. These temperatures and pressures are always higher than those at the Earth's surface and must be sufficiently higher to change the original minerals into other mineral types or recrystallise.

Sandhill

A sandhill is an upland, savanna-like habitat on gently rolling terrain with an open overstory of longleaf pines. This kind of habitat requires frequent, low-intensity fires, about every two to five years, to minimize competition and stimulate flowering and seed germination of many sandhill plants. Monahans Sandhills State Park in Texas, the United States, is an example of a sandhill.

Salt Marsh

A salt marsh is an environment in the upper coastal intertidal zone between land and salty or brackish water. An example of a salt marsh is the Marine Park Salt Marsh Nature Center in New York, the United States.

Scree

A scree is an accumulation of rock fragments at the base of a steep rock slope or cliff. Scree is also called talus. A scree is formed from physical and chemical weathering and erosional processes. It can also be the result of human activity, such as the scree beneath the sculpture of Mount Rushmore in South Dakota, the United States.

Sea

A sea is a large body of salt water. Most seas are connected to or even part of an ocean, but the term can also be used to describe large saline lakes.

Major seas in the Atlantic Ocean:

- Mediterranean Sea – branches from the Atlantic Ocean at the strait of Gibraltar near Spain and Morocco and stretches out between northern Africa and southern Europe until it reaches Lebanon and Israel.
- Baltic Sea – starts from north of Germany until Russia and Finland. The Baltic Sea mainly borders northeastern Europe and Scandinavia.
- Black Sea – branches inland from the Mediterranean Sea by the Straits of Dardanelles and Bosphorus. It is part of the border between Europe and Asia, bordering Bulgaria, Romania, Ukraine, Russia, Georgia, and Turkey.
- Caribbean Sea – branches from the Atlantic Ocean at the Caribbean Islands. The Caribbean Sea's eastern border is the Lesser Antilles while the Greater Antilles makes up its northern border. Central and South America make up the natural borders to the south and west.
- North Sea – lies in between Great Britain and Scandinavia, with Belgium and the Netherlands on the south.

Major seas in the Arctic Ocean:

- Barents Sea – located north of Norway and Russia.
- Beaufort Sea – located north of Alaska, the United States, and Northwest Territories, Canada.
- Bering Sea – located between Alaska, the United States, and Russia. It is north of the Aleutian Islands.
- Kara Sea – located north of Siberia, Russia. It is frozen for most of the year.
- Laptev Sea – located north of Siberia, Russia, east of the Kara Sea.
- East Siberian Sea – located north east of Siberia, Russia, near Alaska, the United States.

Major seas in the Southern Ocean:

- Amundsen Sea – located between Cape Dart and Cape Flying Fish in Antarctica.
- Ross Sea – branches from the Southern Ocean as a deep bay in Antarctica.
- Weddell Sea – the clearest sea in the world. The Weddell Sea is located near Queen Maud Land in Antarctica and is filled with icebergs. It is the 5th largest sea in the world.

Major seas in the Indian Ocean:

- Arabian Sea – branches from the Indian Ocean at the Arabian Peninsula. The Arabian Sea extends inland by the Persian Gulf and the Red Sea. It is the 3rd largest sea in the world.
- Red Sea – branches from the Arabian Sea to separate the Arabian Peninsula of Asia from Africa. It lies on top of the Great Rift Valley.
- Bay of Bengal – the largest bay in the world and often considered a sea. It lies between southeastern India, Bangladesh, and Myanmar.

Major seas in the Pacific Ocean:

- Coral Sea – bounded by Australia in the southwest and Solomon Islands on the north and northeast sides. It is the 2nd largest sea in the world.
- East China Sea – located between mainland China, South Korea, Japan, and Taiwan.
- Philippine Sea – borders Philippines to the east and spans all the way to Japan to the north, and Palau to the east. It is the largest sea in the world.
- Java Sea – located between the islands of Indonesia.
- Sea of Japan – located between the North and South Korea, Russia, and Japan.
- Sea of Okhotsk – surrounded by Russia to the west, north, and east, and Japan to the south.
- South China Sea – starts south of the East China Sea and stretches towards the Malay Peninsula. The South China Sea is bordered to the east by the Philippine Islands. It is the 4th largest sea in the world.

- Sulu Sea – located to the southwest of the Philippine Islands.
- Tasman Sea – located south of the Coral Sea. It is bordered by Australia to the west and New Zealand to the east.
- Yellow Sea – located between China, North Korea, and South Korea. It is north of the East China Sea.

Major landlocked seas (sometimes called lakes) in the world:

- Aral Sea – saline sea on the border between Kazakhstan and Uzbekistan. Since its river sources were irrigated elsewhere by the Soviet Union, the Aral Sea is constantly shrinking, leaving behind salt in the soil.
- Caspian Sea – saline lake that can be considered as an inland sea because of its size and salinity. It is located between Azerbaijan, Iran, Kazakhstan, Russia, and Turkmenistan.
- Dead Sea – saline lake between Israel, West Bank, and Jordan.
- Great Salt Lake – saline lake in Utah, the United States.
- Salton Lake – saline lake in California, the United States.

Sea Cave
A sea cave is a type of cave formed primarily by the wave action of the sea. The waves erode the rock cliff to form an opening that gets gradually deeper. The Cathedral Caves is a series of sea caves in New Zealand.

Sediment
Sediment is the naturally-occurring material that is broken down by processes of weathering and erosion, and is subsequently transported by the action of fluids such as wind, water, or ice, and/or by the force of gravity acting on the particle itself. Sediment can be classified based on its grain size from small to large: colloid, clay, slit, sand, gravel/pebble, cobble, and boulder. Sediment can be found in many places, including riverbeds.

Serac
A serac is a block or column of ice formed by intersecting crevasses on a glacier. It is often house-sized or larger.

Shoal
A shoal is a linear landform within or extending into a body of water typically composed of sand, silt or small pebbles. A shoal can also be called a sandbar or gravebar. An example of a shoal is the tidal shoal that connects the islands of Waya and Wayasewa of the Yasawa Islands in Fiji.

Sinkhole
A sinkhole is a natural depression or hole in the Earth's surface caused by karst processes. A

sinkhole is also called a sink, shake hole, swallow hole, swallet, doline or cenote. The Qattara hole in Egypt is the largest natural sinkhole in the world (50 mi / 80 km long, 75 mi / 120 km wide).

Snowfield
A snowfield is an area of permanent snow accumulation, typically found above the snow line.

Snow Line
The climatic snow line is the point above which snow and ice cover the ground throughout the year. The actual snow line may seasonally be significantly lower. The interplay of altitude and latitude affects the precise placement of the snow line at a particular location. At or near the equator, the snow line is about 15,000 ft (4,500 m); at or near the poles, the snow line is at the sea level.

Sound
A sound is a large bay. A sound is deeper into land than a bight. The Puget Sound in Washington, the United States, is a deep arm of the ocean.

Spit
A spit is a type of shoal, which is a somewhat linear landform within or extending into a body of water. Spits are formed when the longshore drift travels past a point where the dominant drift direction and shoreline do not veer in the same direction. The New Brighton is a spit in New Zealand, created by the longshore drift of sediment from the Waimakariri River.

Spring
A spring is a site where water naturally flows to the surface from underground. Springs are mainly formed when pressure from underground forces water from aquifers, layers of underground water, above ground. Many springs are made possible because of limestone landforms.

Springs are measured by magnitude. The smallest springs are called 8th magnitude springs and release less than one pint of water per minute. The smaller the magnitude of the spring, the more water is released per minute. The largest springs are called 1st magnitude springs and release more than 100 cu ft (2.8 m^3) of water per second.

Springs can release water in several different ways:

- Seepage – small flow as water is filtered through permeable earth.
- Fracture – discharges from fractures in Earth such as faults and fissures.
- Tubular – discharges from cave system.

Notable springs in Europe:

- Aachtopf – the largest natural spring in Germany.
- Castalian Spring – located in Delphi, Greece. The spring used to be where people travelled through to consult the Oracle.
- Fontaine de Vaucluse – located in southwestern France.
- Pierian Spring – located in Greece. The spring has mythological origins as it was supposedly holy to the Muses.
- Spring of Juturna – located in Roman forums, Italy. The ancient Romans built a pool over this spring.

Notable springs in Asia:

- Baotu Spring – a set of 72 springs located in China.
- Gihon Spring – located in Israel. The spring was originally the main water source for ancient Jerusalem.

Notable springs in North America:

- Bennett Spring – located in central Missouri, the United States.
- Big Spring – located in Missouri, the United States. It is one of the largest springs in the world and is getting constantly larger as it melts the limestone that is underneath the spring.
- Blue Spring – located in Florida, the United States. The spring is one of the largest in Florida and is a home to manatees.
- Giant Springs – located in Montana, the United States. The water originates from snowmelt of the Little Belt Mountains.
- Greer Spring – located in Missouri, the United States.
- Mammoth Spring – the largest spring in Arkansas, the United States. The spring is fed by underground water from rainwater.
- Maramec Spring – located in Missouri, the United States.
- Poland Spring – located in Maine, the United States. The water from Poland Spring is currently being used as bottled spring water.
- Kitch-iti-kipi – the largest freshwater spring in Michigan, the United States.
- Rainbow Springs – located in Florida, the United States.
- Saratoga Springs – located in New York, the United States. Surrounding the Saratoga Springs are many other springs, which provide water for nearby towns.
- Silver Springs – located in Florida, the United States. The spring is one of the largest artesian springs in the world.
- Wakulla Springs – located in Florida, the United States. Under the springs are the longest and deepest underwater caves in the world.
- Wekiwa Springs – located in Florida, the United States. The spring provides the water source for the Wekiva River.

Notable spring in South America:

- Guarani Aquifer – located in Brazil. It is one of the largest aquifers in the world and provides water for the surrounding area.

Notable spring in Oceania:

- Te Waikoropupu Springs – located in New Zealand. It has spiritual significance for the Maori people of New Zealand.

Stack

A stack is a landform consisting of a steep and often vertical column or columns of rock in the sea near a coast, isolated by erosion. It is related to stump. The Ball's Pyramid in Australia is the tallest volcanic stack in the world (1,844 ft / 562 m).

Strait

A strait is a narrow, navigable channel of water that connects two larger navigable bodies of water. Sometimes, strait is used interchangeable with channel, firth, passage, and sound.

Major straits in the world:

- Bab el Mandeb – located between Yemen and Eritrea/Djibouti, connecting the Red Sea and the Arabian Sea.
- Bass Strait – located between Tasmania and mainland Australia, connecting the Southern Ocean and the Pacific Ocean.
- Bering Strait – located between Alaska, the United States, and Siberia, Russia, connecting the Pacific Ocean and the Arctic Ocean.
- Bosporus and Dardanelles – located between the Asian Turkey and the European Turkey, connecting the Mediterranean Sea and the Black Sea.
- Cook Strait – located between the North Island and South Island of New Zealand, connecting two parts of the Pacific Ocean.
- Strait of Dover – located between England and France, connecting the North Sea and the English Channel.
- Detroit River – located between the United States and Canada, connecting Lake Saint Clair and Lake Erie.
- Straits of Florida – located between the United States and Cuba, connecting the Gulf of Mexico and the Atlantic Ocean.
- Strait of Gibraltar – located between Spain and Morocco, connecting the Atlantic Ocean and the Mediterranean Sea.
- Strait of Hormuz – located between Iran and United Arab Emirates/Musandam, Oman, connecting the Persian Gulf and the Gulf of Oman.
- Strait of Magellan – located between Tierra del Fuego and mainland Argentina, connecting the Atlantic Ocean and the Pacific Ocean.
- Strait of Malacca – located between mainland Malaysia and Sumatra, Indonesia,

connecting the Indian Ocean with the South China Sea.
- Menai Strait – located between mainland Wales and the island of Anglesey, the United Kingdom, connecting two parts of the North Atlantic Ocean.
- Strait of Messina – located between Calabria and Sicily in Italy, connecting the Tyrrhenian Sea and the Ionian Sea in the Mediterranean Sea.
- Palk Strait – located between India and Sri Lanka, connecting the Bay of Bengal and the Gulf of Mannar.
- Skagerrak, Kattegat, and the Danish straits – located between Norway/Sweden and Denmark, connecting the North Sea to the Baltic Sea.
- Taiwan Strait – located between Taiwan and mainland China, connecting the South China Sea and the East China Sea.
- Pentland Firth – located between the Orkney Islands and mainland Scotland, connecting the North Atlantic Ocean and the North Sea.
- Strait of Georgia – between Vancouver Island and mainland Canada, connecting two parts of the Pacific Ocean.

The Strait of Malacca is the longest strait in the world (500 mi / 805 km).

Stratum
A stratum is a layer of rock or soil with internally consistent characteristics that distinguish it from other layers. Strata are typically seen as bands of different colored or differently structured material exposed in cliffs, road cuts, quarries, and river banks. Different strata can mean that the material in a stratum is a different type of rock or a different age than the stratum above and below it.

Stump
A stump is the collapsed stack caused by erosion. This stump is usually a small rock island, small enough to be submerged by high tide.

Subglacial Mound
A subglacial mound is the type of volcano formed when lava erupts beneath a thick glacier or ice sheet. Subglacial mounds are found throughout Iceland, Antarctica and Canada.

Submarine Canyon
A submarine canyon is a V-shaped valley on the sea floor of a continental slope. Submarine canyons are formed through volcanic activity and can cut down continental slopes at depths of over 1.2 mi (2 km) deep. Some submarine canyons are also found at the edge of the ends of large rivers. The Congo Canyon in the Atlantic Ocean, extending from the Congo River, is the deepest river canyon (1,200 m / 3,900 ft).

Surge Channel
A surge channel is a narrow inlet on a rocky shoreline. Surge channels can range from 4 in (10 cm) across to 10 ft (3 m) or more. The West Coast Trail on the coast of Vancouver

Island, Canada, is famous for its large number of surge channels.

Swamp

A swamp is a type of wetland that is largely flooded. Swamps can have varied vegetation, ranging from grass to trees. They can also contain different types of water such as fresh, saline, or brackish.

Notable swamps in Africa:

- Bangweulu Swamps – the area surrounding Lake Bangweulu in southeastern Zambia. It is a freshwater swamp in the Congo Basin.
- Okavango Swamp – the area that the Okavango River empties out into. The Okavango Swamp is located in Botswana. It is also the largest inland delta in the world, as the water does not flow to sea.
- Sudd – formed by the White Nile. The swamp is located in Sudan. It is one of the largest wetlands in the world.
- Niger Delta – located at the end of the Niger River in Nigeria. The area is currently threatened by pollution due to oil drilling.

Notable swamps in Asia:

- Asmat Swamp – located on the island of New Guinea in Indonesia. It is the largest alluvial swamp in the world.
- Vasyugan Swamp – located in western Siberia in Russia. It is the largest swamp in the northern hemisphere.
- Candaba Swamp – located on the island of Luzon in the Philippines.
- Mangrove Swamp – located in southwestern Pakistan.

Notable swamps in Northern America:

- Atchafalaya National Wildlife Refuge – located in Louisiana, the United States. The refuge is a hardwood swamp, meaning it contains many trees.
- Big Cypress National Preserve – located in Florida, the United States.
- Barley Barber Swamp – located near Lake Okeechobee in Florida, the United States.
- Everglades – located in the southern half of Florida, the United States. Its water is mostly fed by Lake Okeechobee but also has numerous aquifers throughout.
- Great Black Swamp – located in Indiana and Ohio, the United States. The swamp was originally created by glacial activity.
- Great Cypress Swamp – located in Delaware and Maryland, the United States. The swamp is also known as the Great Pocomoke Swamp.
- Great Dismal Swamp – surrounding Lake Drummond in North Carolina and Virginia, the United States.

- Great Swamp National Wildlife Refuge – located in New Jersey, the United States. The swamp is the remnant of a glacial lake.
- Green Swamp (Florida) – located in Florida, the United States.
- Green Swamp (North Carolina) – located in North Carolina, the United States. The swamp is one of the natural habitats of the Venus Fly Trap.
- Honey Island Swamp – located in Louisiana, the United States. The swamp is one of the most untouched swamps in the United States.
- Hudson Bay Lowlands – located in Canada near the Hudson and James Bays.
- Limberlost – located in Indiana, the United States.
- Mingo National Wildlife Refuge – located in Missouri, the United States. The swamp borders Lake Wappapello, which is the water source of the swamp.
- Okefenokee Swamp – located in Georgia and Florida, the United States. The swamp is the largest peat swamp in the United States and one of the largest swamps in the world.
- Reelfoot Lake – a shallow lake surrounded by swampland in Tennessee and Kentucky, the United States.
- Shu Swamp – located in New York, the United States.

Notable swamps in Southern America:

- Lahuen Ñadi – located in Chile
- Pantanal – located in Brazil, Bolivia, and Paraguay. It is one of the largest wetlands in the world.
- Paraná Delta – located at the end of the Parana River in Argentina.

Swash
Swash is the water that washes up on shore after an incoming wave has broken. It is opposite to backwash.

Table
A table is a hill, flank of a mountain, or mountain, which has a flat top. This landform has numerous names in addition to table: tuya, mesa, tepui, potrero, butte, plateau, and terrace.

Tea Table
A tea table is a type of rock column comprising discrete strata layers, usually of sedimentary rock, with the top layers being wider than the base due to greater resistance to erosion and weathering. The Devils Tea Table is located in Ohio, the United States.

Tepui
A tepui is a table-top mountain or mesa found in the Guiana Highlands of South America, especially in Venezuela. The Mount Roraima is the highest of the Pakaraima chain of tepui

plateau in South America (9,219 ft / 2,810 m).

Terrace
A terrace is a step-like, elevated surface landform above the existing level of a floodplain or fluvial valleys.

Terraces can be classified based on the environments:

- Fluvial Terrace – an elongated terrace that flanks the sides of floodplains and fluvial valleys, which exist all over the world.
- Marine Terrace – former shorelines of seas or oceans.
- Lake (Tacustrine) Terrace – former shorelines of either a nonglacial, glacial, or proglacial lake
- Structural Terrace – a terrace created by the differential erosion of flat-lying or nearly flat-lying layered strata.

Topography
Topography is the study of the terrain of Earth's surface. Topography is mainly used to show the elevation changes of the land, especially during a slope of a hill or other uneven land.

Tornado
A tornado is a violent column of wind that stretches from a cumulonimbus cloud to the ground. Tornadoes occur on every continent in the world except for Antarctica, but the majority of tornadoes occur in North America. A tornado's strength is measured by the Fujita scale, from F0 which is harmless to F5 where wind speed is so high that any building is threatened.

Types of tornadoes:

- Normal – the classic tornado, with a column of wind varying in size and height.
- Multiple vortex – there are sometimes two or more tornadoes at the same place. This typically occurs when the wind speed is very high.
- Waterspout – a tornado that occurs over water. Instead of wind, the column consists of water.
- Landspout – a tornado consisting of dust rather than wind. Landspouts tend to be weak as well as short living.

Tombolo
A tombolo is a strip usually made of sand that links an island to the mainland or to another island, formed by deposition when waves are refracted round the island. There is a tombolo in Tuscany, Italy.

Tropical Cyclone
A tropical cyclone is a storm system that contains a large low pressure center surrounded by thunderstorms. The center, sometimes containing an eye, will be calm while the surrounding storms gush out torrential rain and wind. The area around the center rotates clockwise in the southern hemisphere and counterclockwise in the northern hemisphere.

Types of tropical cyclones:

- Tropical depression – a tropical cyclone with winds below 38 mi (61 km) per hour. There are usually no eyes.
- Tropical storm – a tropical cyclone with winds between 39 mi (63 km) and 73 mi (117 km) per hour. There is sometimes an eye in the center of a tropical storm.
- Hurricane – a tropical cyclone with winds of at least 74 mi (119 km) per hour. There is usually an eye in a hurricane. The term hurricane is usually used in the Northeast Pacific and North Atlantic Oceans.
- Typhoon – a tropical cyclone with the same characteristics as a hurricane. The term is used in the Northwest Pacific Ocean.

Tuya
A tuya is a type of distinctive, flat-topped, steep-sided volcano formed when lava erupts through a thick glacier or ice sheet.

Tuya examples:

- Brown Bluff in Antarctica
- Tuya Butte in Canada
- Tuya Volcanic Field in Canada
- The Table in Canada
- Hayrick Butte in Oregon, the United States
- Hogg Rock in Oregon, the United States
- Herðubreið in Iceland
- Hlöðufell in Iceland

Vale
A Vale is a wide river valley. A vale usually occurs between two chalk domes where the ground has been eroded into clay. The most notable vale would be the Kashmir Valley, the disputed territory between India and Pakistan.

Valley
A valley is a depression with predominant extent in one direction. A very deep river valley may be called a canyon. A valley is called a dale in the lowlands of Scotland, the United Kingdom.

Types of valleys:

- U-shaped valley – U-shaped, formed by the process of glaciation. U-shaped valleys occur in the Alps and Rocky Mountains.
- V-shaped valley – V-shaped, formed by flowing water. Black Canyon of Gunnison National Park and Grand Canyon National Park in the United States are examples of V-shaped valleys.
- Rift valley – linear-shaped, formed by the action of a geologic rift or fault. The Great Rift Valley in Eastern Africa is an example of a rift valley.

Notable valleys in the world:

- Aburra Valley in Colombia
- Cauca Valley in Colombia
- Barossa Valley in Australia
- Hunter Valley in Australia
- Central Valley in California, the United States
- Death Valley in California, the United States
- Grand Canyon in Arizona, the United States
- Las Vegas Valley in Nevada, the United States
- Little Cottonwood Creek Valley in Utah, the United States
- Napa Valley in California, the United States
- Palo Duro Canyon in Texas, the United States
- Rio Grande Valley in Texas, the United States
- San Fernando Valley in California, the United States
- Silicon Valley, in California, the United States
- Sonoma Valley in California, the United States
- Valley of the Sun in Arizona, the United States
- Willamette Valley in Oregon, the United States
- Danube Valley in Eastern Europe
- Fraser Canyon in Canada
- Fraser Valley in Canada
- Hell's Gate in Canada
- Okanagan Valley in Canada
- Ottawa Valley in Canada
- Saint Lawrence Valley in Canada
- Glen Coe in the United Kingdom
- Great Glen in the United Kingdom
- Nant Ffrancon in the United Kingdom
- South Wales Valleys in the United Kingdom
- Great Rift Valley in Eastern Africa
- Hutt Valley in New Zealand
- Indus Valley in Pakistan

- Iron Gate in Romania and Serbia
- Loire Valley in France
- Upper Rhine Valley in France
- Rhone Valley in France
- Nile Valley in Northeast Africa
- Panjshir Valley in Afghanistan
- Valley of Flowers in India
- Valley of the Kings in Egypt
- Valley of Mexico in Mexico

The largest and longest valley in the world is the Great Rift Valley (26,830 sq mi / 69,490 km^2, 3,700 mi / 6,000 km), formed by plate tectonics. The largest valley formed by erosion in the world is California's Central Valley in the United States (22,500 sq mi / 58,275 km^2).

Ventifact

Ventifact is a rock that has been abraded, pitted, etched, grooved, or polished by wind-driven sand or ice crystals. Ventifacts are often found in the desert pavement. Ventifacts can be used to determine the wind direction at the time that they were created.

Volcanic Arc

A volcanic arc is a chain of volcanoes parallel to a mountain belt positioned in an arc shape as seen from above. The volcanic arc is called an oceanic arc when a volcanic island arc is formed. The Sunda Arc is an oceanic arc that formed the islands of Sumatra, Java, the Sunda Strait and the Lesser Sunda Islands in Indonesia. The volcanic arc is called a continental arc when an arc-shaped mountain belt is formed. The Cascade Volcanic Arc is a continental arc that has formed a number of volcanoes in western North America.

Volcanic Complex

A volcanic complex is a collection of related volcanoes or volcanic landforms. A volcanic complex is also called a volcanic group.

Notable volcanic complexes in the world:

- Akan Volcanic Complex – a group of volcanoes in Japan that grew out of the Akan caldera, located in Akan National Park on the island of Hokkaido.
- Antillanca Group – a group of scoria cones, maars and small stratovolcanoes in Chile, mostly located in Puyehue National Park.
- Azuma Group – a group of volcanic lakes in Japan, including Goshiki-numa, the "Five Colored Lakes".
- Banda Islands – a group of 10 small volcanic islands in the Banda Sea, Indonesia.
- Blake River Megacaldera Complex – a nested caldera system in Canada.
- Borrowdale Volcanic Group – a group of lavas, tuffs and agglomerates, and some major igneous intrusions in the United Kingdom.

- Carmacks Group – a group of flood basalts, coarse volcaniclastic rocks, sandy tuffs, and lava flows in Canada.
- Carrán-Los Venados – a group of scoria cones, maars and small stratovolcanoes in Chile.
- Cochiquito Volcanic Group – a group of volcanoes in Argentina, including the main peak, Volcán Cochiquito (stratovolcano), and 8 satellite cones in the volcanic field.
- Coppermine River Group – large flood basalt in Canada.
- Dacht-i-Navar Group – a group of 15 lava domes in Afghanistan.
- Daisetsuzan Volcanic Group – a group of mountain peaks in Ohachi-Daira caldera, located in Daisetsuzan National Park, Japan.
- Duluth Complex – a group of intrusive rocks, including Beaver Bay Complex, adjoined and interspersed with the extrusive rocks of the North Shore Volcanic Group. It is located in Minnesota, the United States.
- Ellesmere Island Volcanics – a group of volcanoes and lava flows in Canada.
- Fueguino – a group of lava domes and pyroclastic cones located on Cook Island, Chile.
- Galápagos Islands – an archipelago of volcanic islands, located in Galápagos National Park, Ecuador.
- Gambier Group – a prehistoric volcanic arc in Canada.
- Hakkōda Mountains – more than a dozen stratovolcanoes and lava domes arranged into two volcanic groups in Japan.
- Heard and McDonald Islands – 2 active volcanoes in Australia.
- Jemez Mountains – a volcanism, consisting of a broadly circular ridge surrounding the Valles Caldera. It is located in New Mexico, the United States.
- Kaiserstuhl – a volcano mountain range in Germany.
- Karpinsky Group – 2 volcanic cones, on Paramushir Island of Kuril Islands, Russia.
- Lomonosov Group – a group of cinder cones, on Paramushir Island of Kuril Islands, Russia.
- Meager Group – the most unstable volcanic massif in Canada.
- Milbanke Sound Group – a group of 5 small basaltic volcanoes in Canada.
- Monti della Tolfa – a volcanic group in the Anti-Apennines in Central Italy.
- Mount Edziza volcanic complex – a complex active volcano in Canada.
- Mount Raiden Volcanic Group – a group of active volcanoes on Hokkaido, Japan.
- Nipesotsu-Maruyama Volcanic Group – a group of stratovolcanoes and lava domes on Hokkaido, Japan.
- Niseko Volcanic Group – an active group of volcanoes on Hokkaido, younger than most other volcanic groups on Hokkaido, Japan.
- Northern Yatsugatake Volcanic Group – a group of volcanoes on Honshu, Japan.
- Olkoviy Volcanic Group – a group of volcanoes on the Kamchatka Peninsula, Russia.
- Pinacate Peaks – active cinder cones and volcanic peaks in Mexico.
- Pocdol Mountains – an active group of stratovolcanoes in the Philippines.
- Puyuhuapi – a volcanic group of cinder cones in Chile.
- Rat Islands – a volcanic island chain in the Aleutian Islands, the United States.

- Shikaribetsu Volcanic Group – a volcanic group of lava domes on Hokkaido, Japan.
- Skukum Group – a group of calderas in Canada.
- Southern Yatsugatake Volcanic Group in Japan – a group of inactive volcanoes.
- Spences Bridge Group – a group of shield volcanoes and stratovolcanoes located in Canada.
- Takuan Group – a group of 3 stratovolcanoes located in Papua New Guinea.
- Tatun Volcano Group – a group of volcanoes in northern Taiwan, China.
- Tokachi Volcanic Group – a group of mainly stratovolcanoes in Japan.
- Tomuraushi Volcanic Group – a group of stratovolcanoes and lava domes located in Japan.
- Tristan da Cunha – a volcanic chain of islands, and the most remote inhabited islands in the world. It is located in the United Kingdom.
- Vernadskii Ridge – a group of islands on the Kuril Islands, Russia.
- Vitu Islands – a volcanic island group in Papua New Guinea.
- Yasawa Group – a group of 20 volcanic islands in Fiji.

Volcanic Cone

A volcanic cone is built by ejecta from a volcanic vent, piling up around the vent in the shape of a cone with a central crater.

Volcanic cones can be classified by the nature and size of the fragments ejected during the eruption:

- Stratocone – a large cylindrical structure built up around a main tubular volcanic vent by more than one eruption. Osorno volcano in Chile is an example of a stratocone.
- Spatter cone – formed of molten lava ejected from a vent somewhat like taffy. There are spatter cones in Craters of Moon National Monument, Idaho, the United States
- Ash cone – composed of ejected small particles called ash.
- Tuff Cone – a consolidated ash cone. Diamond Head in Hawaii, the United States, is an example of a tuff cone.
- Cinder cone (also called scoria cone) – built almost entirely of loose volcanic fragments called cinders (pumice, pyroclastics, or tephra). Sunset Crater in Sunset Crater Volcano National Monument in Arizona, the United States is an example of a cinder cone.
- Rootless Cone – also called pseudocrater.

Volcanic Crater

A volcanic crater is a circular depression in the ground caused by volcanic activity. If the volcano's magma chamber is empty enough for an area above it to subside, it forms a caldera. If the volcanic crater fills with rain and/or melted snow, it forms a crater lake.

Volcanic Dam

A volcanic dam is a natural dam produced by volcanic activity. The Barrier is a lava dam that impounds the Garibaldi Lake in Canada.

Volcanic Field

A volcanic field is an area of the Earth's crust that is prone to localized volcanic activity. They usually contain 10 to 100 volcanoes.

Notable volcanic fields in the world:

- Atlin Volcanic Field – a group of cinder cones in Canada.
- Desolation Lava Field – a group of shield volcanoes, calderas, lava domes, stratovolcanoes, cinder cones, and lava flows in Canada.
- Garibaldi Lake Volcanic Field – 9 small stratovolcanoes and lava flows in Canada.
- Mount Cayley Volcanic Field – a group of stratovolcanoes, subglacial volcanoes, and lava flows in Canada.
- Tuya Volcanic Field – a group of tuyas, shield volcanoes, postglacial cones, cinder cones, and lava flows in Canada.
- Wells Gray-Clearwater Volcanic Field – a group of tuyas, ice-ponded valley deposits, subglacial mounds, cinder cones, subaqueous volcanos, lava flows, pit craters, crater lakes, rivers, and waterfalls in the Wells Gray Provincial Park, Canada.
- Wrangell Volcanic Field – a group of shield volcanoes, stratovolcanoes, caldera complexes, cinder cones, and lava flows in Canada and Alaska, the United States.
- Boring Lava Field – 32 cinder cones and small shield volcanoes in Oregon, the United States.
- Clear Lake Volcanic Field – a group of lava domes, cinder cones, and maars in California, the United States.
- Coso Volcanic Field – a group of lava domes and the Fossil Falls in California, the United States.
- Indian Heaven – 7 small shield volcanoes in Washington, the United States.
- Marysvale Volcanic Field – a group of stratovolcanoes, calderas, lava domes, and cinder cones in Utah, the United States.
- Raton-Clayton Volcanic Field – a group of extinct volcanoes including the Capulin Volcano National Monument in New Mexico, the United States.
- San Francisco Volcanic Field – 600 volcanoes, vents, and lava domes in Arizona, the United States.
- Taos Plateau Volcanic Field – a group of sheet flows, cinder cones, shield volcanoes, lava flows, and vents in New Mexico, the United States.
- Cu-Lao Re Group – 13 volcanic cones in Vietnam.
- Meidob Volcanic Field – 316 cinder cones, lave flows, lava domes, tuff cones, maars, and 700 eruptive vents in Sudan.
- Auckland Volcanic Field – dominant, a group of explosion craters, scoria cones, and lava flows on the North Island of New Zealand.

- Haruj – 150 volcanoes (numerous scoria cones and 30 small shield volcanoes), craters, and lava flows in Libya.

Volcano

A volcano is an opening in the Earth's crust where magma can spill out. Volcanoes are most commonly found in breaks in tectonic plates, as there are holes to allow the magma out.

Types of volcanoes:

- Fissure vent – a flat linear crack where lava flows through.
- Shield volcano – a large shield-like volcano. Eruptions from this type of volcano are smooth, and add to the large size of the volcano even more as the lava will cool down on the slope rather than explode into the air.
- Cryptodome – a bulge in land caused by pressure from lava. When it collapses, an eruption will occur.
- Cinder cone – a cone that tends to erupt only once in its lifetime. The shape of the volcano resembles cinders.
- Stratovolcano – a tall cone-like volcano that can have violent eruptions. Mount Fuji in Japan and Mount Vesuvius in Italy are stratovolcanoes.
- Supervolcano – a very large volcano, usually with a caldera. Supervolcanoes have the biggest eruptions out of all the volcano types. An eruption from this type of volcano can change the short term climate of the entire planet. The Yellowstone Caldera in Yellowstone National Park, the United States, is a supervolcano.
- Submarine volcano – an opening on the ocean floor that expels steam and lava into the sea. Because they are under the ocean, submarine volcanoes are not noticeable except in shallow water.
- Subglacial volcano – a volcano that develops under a glacier. When the glacier melts, the lava at the top will collapse, leaving behind a cone missing its top.

There are 16 decade volcanoes, volcanoes that have a potential for a large eruption and is close to a populated area:

- Avachinsky- Koryaksky – a pair of active stratovolcanoes located on the Kamchatka peninsula in eastern Russia.
- Nevado de Colima – a pair of stratovolcanoes, one extinct and one active, located in western Mexico.
- Mount Etna – an active stratovolcano located on the island of Sicily, Italy. It is the tallest active volcano in Europe.
- Galeras – an active stratovolcano in Colombia.
- Mauna Loa – an active shield volcano on the Big Island of Hawaii, the United States. It is the largest volcano on Earth by volume.
- Mount Merapi – an active stratovolcano on the island of Java, Indonesia.
- Mount Nyiragongo – an active volcano on the far eastern side of the Democratic Republic of the Congo. It is part of the Great Rift Valley.

- Mount Rainier – a very large active stratovolcano consisting of three different summits in Washington, the United States.
- Sakurajima – an active stratovolcano consisting of three different summits on the island of Kyushu, Japan. Sakurajima used to be an island before the lava flows of an eruption in 1914 connected it to Kyushu.
- Santa Maria/Santiaguito – an active stratovolcano in western Guatemala.
- Santorini – an island and also a caldera volcano in Greece.
- Taal Volcano – a complex volcano on the island of Luzon, the Philippines. It is very close to the capital, Manila.
- Teide – an active stratovolcano on the Canary Islands. It is the highest point of Spain.
- Ulawun – an active stratovolcano on the island of New Britain, Papua New Guinea.
- Mount Unzen – a group of active stratovolcanoes on the island of Kyushu, Japan.
- Mount Vesuvius – an active somma volcano in Italy. It is the most recently active volcano on mainland Europe.

Waterfall

A waterfall is a place where flowing water rapidly drops in elevation as it flows over a steep region or a cliff. The Angel Falls in Venezuela is the tallest waterfall in the world (3,212 ft / 979 m).

Types of waterfalls:

- Block / Sheet – water descends from a relatively wide stream or river. The Chase Creek Falls in Canada is an example of a block fall.
- Cascade / Multi-Cascading – water descends a series of rock steps. The Rocky Run Falls in Washington, the United States, is an example of a cascade fall.
- Cataract – large and powerful water rushes down with force. The Snoqualmie Falls in Washington, the United States, is an example of a cataract.
- Chute – a large quantity of water forces through a narrow, vertical passage. The Panther Falls in Canada is an example of a chute fall.
- Classical – similar to a block fall, water drops over a ledge but is almost equal in width and height. The Dundas Falls in Canada is an example of a classical fall.
- Combination – many waterfalls are a combination of more than one type of falls. The Paulina Creek Falls in Oregon, the United States is an example of a combination fall.
- Curtain – similar to a block fall or a classical fall, water drops over a ledge. It is taller than its width but not as narrow as a ribbon fall. The Ammonite Falls in Canada is an example of a curtain fall.
- Dry / Historic – this type of fall no longer has water flowing over it. The Dry Falls in Washington, the United States, is an example of a dry fall.
- Fan – water falls through a relatively narrow crest and spreads out, and becomes

wider as it descends. The Hardy Falls in Canada is an example of a fan fall.
- Frozen – this type of fall has ice as a part of the fall. The Hardy Falls in Canada is an example of a frozen fall.
- Horsetail – descending water maintains some contact with bedrock. The Tulip Creek Falls in Canada is an example of a horsetail fall.
- Keyhole / Slot – water pushes through a narrow area before falling. The Spahats Creek Falls in Canada is an example of a keyhole fall.
- Ledge – water falls from a cliff that is relatively flat with some width at the top and is vertical or almost vertical. The Angel Falls in Venezuela is an example of a ledge fall.
- Overhanging ledge – water falls from a cliff that water has eroded underneath it, causing an obvious overhang resulting in the water free falling to the surface below. The Blackwater Falls in West Virginia, the United States, is an example of an overhanging ledge fall.
- Parallel / Twin – two or more falls occur side-by-side and fall similar to each other. The Naramata Falls in Canada is an example of a parallel fall.
- Plunge / Vertical – water descends vertically, losing contact with bedrock surface. The Roaring Creek Falls in Washington, the United States, is an example of a plunge fall.
- Punchbowl – water descends in a constricted form and then spreads out in a wider pool. The Punchbowl Falls in Canada is an example of a punchbowl fall.
- Ribbon – water descends in a narrow strip significantly taller than its width. The Bridal Veil Falls in Canada is an example of a ribbon fall.
- Segmented – the descending water is segmented into distinctive flows by land. The Rocky Creek Falls in Oregon, the United States, is an example of a segmented fall.
- Scree / Talus – water flows over a scree, a chaotic mix of rock debris on a slope usually found at the base of a cliff. The Lyle Creek Falls in Canada is an example of a scree fall.
- Slide – water glides over a single slab of rock maintaining smooth continuous contact. The Shannon Falls in Canada is an example of a slide fall.
- Tiered / Staircase / Multi-Stepped – water drops in a series of distinct steps or falls. The Tangle Creek Falls in Canada is an example of a tiered fall.
- Veil – water drops overlarge rocks creating a thin layer of water that just barely covers its surface. The Bridal Veil Falls in Canada is an example of a veil fall.

Notable waterfalls in the world:

- Angel Falls – the tallest waterfall in the world (3,212 ft / 979 m). It is located in Venezuela over the edge of the Auyantepui Mountain.
- Tugela Falls – the 2nd tallest waterfall in the world (3,107 ft / 947 m). It is located in South Africa.
- Ramnefjellsfossen – the 3rd tallest waterfall in the world (2,651 ft / 808 m). It is located in Norway.
- Victoria Falls – the largest waterfall by size in the world (width: 5,604 ft / 1,708 m,

height: 354 ft / 108 m). It is located on the border of Zimbabwe and Zambia.
- Gocta Cataracs – the tallest waterfall in Peru.
- Hannoki Falls – the tallest waterfall in Asia (1,640 ft / 500 m). It is located in Japan.
- Niagara Falls – one of the most famous waterfalls in the world. It is considered to be the most powerful falls in North America. It is located on the border of Canada and the United States.
- Waihilau Falls – the tallest waterfall of North America (2,600 ft / 792 m). It is located in Hawaii, the United States.
- Yosemite Falls – the 2nd tallest waterfall of North America (2,425 ft / 739 m). It is located in California, the United States.

Water Salinity
Water can be clarified by its salinity, the saltiness. Geographically, the term water salinity is typically used to describe the water type of a body of water.

Classifications of water salinity:

- Freshwater – Water salinity < 0.5 ‰. The naturally water in bogs, ponds, lakes, rivers and streams are freshwater.
- Brackish water – Water salinity is 0.5 – 30 ‰. The Baltic Sea in Europe is a brackish sea.
- Saline water – Water salinity is 30 – 50 ‰. The sea water is saline water.
- Brine water – Water salinity is > 50 ‰. There is no natural brine water.

Watershed
A watershed is an area where many water sources come together. The water is mostly consisted of small streams of rain or melting snow. The resulting water will go on to form rivers. The term can also be used to refer to the divide that separates different watersheds from each other.

Wave-Cut Platform
A wave-cut platform is a flat or slightly sloping bedrock surface that forms in the tidal zone, caused by the wave erosion. There is a wave-cut platform at the beach of Southerndown, the United Kingdom.

Wetland
A wetland is an area where the soil is usually or always saturated with water. Because of the excess water, wetlands are usually covered by pools.

There are many types of wetlands: swamp, marsh, bog, vernal pool, and slough.

Wind
Wind is the movement of air. Wind occurs mostly when there is a difference of

temperatures, most often between air over the sea and the air over land. There are varying degrees of wind, from a breeze to a hurricane. It is measured by the Beaufort Scale, where 0 means no or almost no wind, to 17, which is a very strong hurricane.

Yardang

A yardang is a streamlined hill carved from bedrock or any consolidated or semi-consolidated material by the dual action of wind abrasion, dust and sand, and deflation. Yardangs vary in sizes.

The categories for yardangs are differentiated by size:

- Mega-yardangs – the largest yardangs. They can be several miles or kilometers long and many meters high.
- Meso-yardang – medium sized yardangs. They can be a few feet or meters high and wide.
- Micro-yardangs – the smallest yardangs. They can be a few inches or centimeters high or wide.

Yardangs can be found in most deserts on the earth. A lot of mega-yardangs are located in Tibesti Mountains of the Sahara Desert. Some notable yardangs are "Hole in the Rock" and Window Rock in Arizona, the United States.

Bibliography

- Answers.com – Online Dictionary, Encyclopedia and much more, http://www.answers.com/
- Background Notes, http://www.state.gov/r/pa/ei/bgn/
- Canada's Aquatic Environments, http://www.aquatic.uoguelph.ca/
- China Virtual Museums, http://www.kepu.net.cn/english/canyon/hiking/hik301.html
- CIA – The World Factbook, https://www.cia.gov/library/publications/the-world-factbook/
- Dictionary and Thesaurus – Merriam-Webster Online, http://www.merriam-webster.com/
- Factoidz, http://factoidz.com/
- Geography Page, http://peakbagger.com/
- Geography Summaries Index – Vaughn's Summaries, http://www.vaughns-1-pagers.com/geography/
- Infoplease: Encyclopedia, Almanac, Atlas, Biographies, Dictionary, Thesaurus. Free online reference, research & homework help, http://www.infoplease.com/
- Jarroux Zangbo Grand Canyon, http://baike.baidu.com/view/38822.htm
- National Snow and Ice Data Center (NSIDC) – http://nsidc.org/
- NSS GEO2 Committee On Long And Deep Caves, http://www.caverbob.com
- PhysicalGeography.net, http://www.physicalgeography.net/
- Wikipedia – The Free Encyclopedia, http://en.wikipedia.org/wiki/Main_Page
- World Atlas of Maps Flags and Geography Facts and Figures, http://www.worldatlas.com/
- Worldwaterfalls.com – http://worldwaterfalls.com/

Other Books

- World Geography Questionnaires: Americas – Countries and Territories in the Region (Volume 1), Kenneth Ma and Jennifer Fu, ISBN-10: 1449553222, ISBN-13: 978-1449553227
- World Geography Questionnaires: Africa – Countries and Territories in the Region (Volume 2), Kenneth Ma and Jennifer Fu, ISBN-10: 1451587074, ISBN-13: 978-1451587074
- World Geography Questionnaires: Oceania & Antarctica – Countries and Territories in the Region (Volume 3), Kenneth Ma and Jennifer Fu, ISBN-10: 1453665250, ISBN-13: 978-1453665251
- World Geography Questionnaires: Asia – Countries and Territories in the Region (Volume 4), Kenneth Ma and Jennifer Fu, ISBN-10: 1453831983, ISBN-13: 978-1453831984
- World Geography Questionnaires: Europe – Countries and Territories in the Region (Volume 5), Kenneth Ma and Jennifer Fu, ISBN-10: 1453833498, ISBN-13: 978-1453833490
- World Geography Questionnaires: United States Geography Questionnaires (Volume 7), Kenneth Ma and Jennifer Fu, ISBN-10: 1477408673, ISBN-13: 978-1477408674
- The Missing Mau, Hermione Ma and Jennifer Fu, ISBN-10: 1451587090, ISBN-13: 978-1451587098
- The Crazy College, Hermione Ma and Jennifer Fu, ISBN-10: 1452851174, ISBN-13: 978-1452851174
- The Revolving Resort, Hermione Ma and Jennifer Fu, ISBN-10: 1453815139, ISBN-13: 978-1453815137
- The Gingerbread Museum of Candy, Omelets, Spinach, Ice, and Biscuits, Hermione Ma, ISBN-10: 1477543252, ISBN-13: 978-1477543252
- ACE Your Java Interview, Jennifer Fu, ISBN-10: 1484104935, ISBN-13: 978-1484104934
- Bubble, Jennifer Fu, ISBN-10: 1461029120, ISBN-13: 978-1461029120

About the Authors

Kenneth Ma is a twelfth grader at Monta Vista High School in Cupertino, California. He was the National Geography School Bee at Eaton Elementary School in Cupertino when he was in fourth grade, and he was the National Geography School Bee at Kennedy Middle School in Cupertino when he was in sixth grade. He was also a member of the Kennedy Middle School National Geography Challenge Championship team in 2007. In 2007, he was honored with the Outstanding Achievement in Geography Award from his middle school. Besides his interest in Geography, Kenneth is also an avid soccer player.

Jennifer Fu is Kenneth's mom and lives in Cupertino, California. She is a software engineer by day and an aspiring writer by night. She has contributed short stories and novellas to a number of on-line publications in Chinese. Writing a geography book is a new endeavor for her.

Made in the USA
Coppell, TX
05 December 2020